Cambridge Elements

Elements in the Philosophy of Biology
edited by
Grant Ramsey
KU Leuven

PHILOSOPHY OF PHYSIOLOGY

Maël Lemoine
University of Bordeaux

Shaftesbury Road, Cambridge CB2 8EA, United Kingdom

One Liberty Plaza, 20th Floor, New York, NY 10006, USA

477 Williamstown Road, Port Melbourne, VIC 3207, Australia

314–321, 3rd Floor, Plot 3, Splendor Forum, Jasola District Centre,
New Delhi – 110025, India

103 Penang Road, #05–06/07, Visioncrest Commercial, Singapore 238467

Cambridge University Press is part of Cambridge University Press & Assessment,
a department of the University of Cambridge.

We share the University's mission to contribute to society through the pursuit of
education, learning and research at the highest international levels of excellence.

www.cambridge.org
Information on this title: www.cambridge.org/9781009486583

DOI: 10.1017/9781009370394

© Maël Lemoine 2025

This publication is in copyright. Subject to statutory exception and to the provisions
of relevant collective licensing agreements, no reproduction of any part may take
place without the written permission of Cambridge University Press & Assessment.

When citing this work, please include a reference to the DOI 10.1017/9781009370394

First published 2025

A catalogue record for this publication is available from the British Library

ISBN 978-1-009-48658-3 Hardback
ISBN 978-1-009-37037-0 Paperback
ISSN 2515-1126 (online)
ISSN 2515-1118 (print)

Cambridge University Press & Assessment has no responsibility for the persistence
or accuracy of URLs for external or third-party internet websites referred to in this
publication and does not guarantee that any content on such websites is, or will
remain, accurate or appropriate.

Philosophy of Physiology

Elements in the Philosophy of Biology

DOI: 10.1017/9781009370394
First published online: January 2025

Maël Lemoine
University of Bordeaux

Author for correspondence: Maël Lemoine, mael.lemoine@u-bordeaux.fr

Abstract: Time is ripe to complement the question "what is health and disease?" in philosophy of medicine with a "philosophy of physiology." Indeed, the actors in this debate share the conviction that a "foundational" concept dictates to this scientific field what is to be considered healthy or pathological and leaves it to explore only facts and mechanisms. Rejecting this presupposition, philosophy of physiology accepts that biomedical sciences explore and redefine their own object: the healthy, the pathological. Indeed, various theories of disease and health, that philosophers have rarely studied, form the core of biomedical research, too hastily considered as a science "without theories." The Element identifies them, and clarifies their content, presuppositions, and scope. Finally, it proposes a new question about the unity of the pathological phenomenon: not "what do all diseases have in common?" but rather, "why is the susceptibility to disease a universal and necessary characteristic of living beings?"

Keywords: health, disease, physiology, medicine, evolution

© Maël Lemoine 2025

ISBNs: 9781009486583 (HB), 9781009370370 (PB), 9781009370394 (OC)
ISSNs: 2515-1126 (online), 2515-1118 (print)

Contents

1 From Philosophy of Medicine to Philosophy of Physiology   1

2 Disease Entities and Pathophysiological Processes   17

3 How Generalizable Are Disease Theories?   27

4 Toward a Theory of the Pathological Phenomenon   41

5 Toward a Theory of Physiological Health   53

6 Conclusion   67

   References   69

1 From Philosophy of Medicine to Philosophy of Physiology

A huge body of scientific literature describes how organisms function – how bacteria reproduce, how photosynthesis happens, how bears survive during hibernation, how humans sleep – as well as how they *typically* dysfunction via infection, dehydration, starvation, insomnia, scurvy, diabetes, cancer, multiple sclerosis, and so on. The former is called "physiology," the latter "pathophysiology," though both are typically subsumed within an expansive understanding of "physiology." Physiology (in this broader sense) is not an exclusively medical science, but it certainly is a core science for medicine. As with any other science, physiology is likely to raise conceptual problems. For instance, why are some bacteria called "pathogens" if they never produce symptoms or shorten lifespan in some individuals? Is cancer one or many diseases? What does it mean for an organism to "repair itself"? Is disease a universal and necessary fact of life? How can we measure degrees of "health," are there mechanisms of health, and what exactly is the difference between health and fitness? If you are interested in these questions, it seems natural to turn to philosophy of medicine. But this section argues that this is not the best place to start. Instead, it proposes an alternative approach, one centered on the philosophy of physiology, and argues that this is a better path to understanding health and disease.

1.1 A Short Overview of the Health and Disease Debate in Philosophy of Medicine

If you are diagnosed with major depressive disorder, you may protest and argue that in fact, *the world* is depressing and that *you* are not sick – only lucid. Psychiatrists would be encouraged to label this behavior "poor insight" (that is, a weak degree of the patient's awareness of their symptoms). On the Hamilton Depression Rating Scale, a standard tool in psychiatry, that would be a sign of the severity of the disease. This is just one of the many examples where doctors seem to be entitled to decide *factually* how you should be treated. What justifies such authority of medical science?

Sociologists have *described* the social process that leads to this authority, and called it "medicalization" (Conrad 2007), that is, the social consensus that a problem should be dealt with by medicine. In philosophy of medicine, the question raised is the *justification* of this authority. This question has been interpreted as a question of definition. Indeed, with a correct definition of health and disease, we would have criteria to decide what really is a disease.

In recent history, philosophers of medicine have polarized into two camps:

- *Naturalists* define "health" and "disease" in terms of biological functions and dysfunctions. The knowledge of biological facts justifies that you have a disease (or not).
- *Normativists* claim that "health" and "disease" definitions reflect social values. The observation of what is deemed to be "harmful" in a society justifies that you are judged sick (or not).

This alternative is deeply ingrained in the health and disease debate: most contributions in philosophy of medicine dealing with the definition of disease either endorse, reject, or combine these positions.

Undoubtedly, the champion of *naturalism* is Christopher Boorse. His seminal paper, "Health as a Theoretical Concept" (Boorse 1977), has both initiated this debate and proposed a complete, naturalistic definition of health. It is called the "Biostatistical Theory of health and disease" (BST). According to the BST, "Theoretical health (...) is the absence of disease; disease is only statistically species-subnormal biological part-function; therefore, the classification of human states as healthy or diseased is an objective matter, to be read off the biological facts of nature without need of value judgments" (Boorse 1997). In other terms, physiology determines the nature and statistically normal level of efficiency of all functions of the parts of an organism in a given species, or, more precisely, in the various "reference classes" in a species – that is, mainly, groups defined by being either male or female and child, adult or elderly. Thus, basic concepts of physiology determine the generic criteria for specific conditions to be considered real diseases.

Although a majority of articles endorse *normativism*, there is no dominant version of normativism. Some forms of normativism draw criteria of health and disease either from values (Engelhardt 1996), requirements of human action (Clouser et al. 1981), or conditions for happiness (Nordenfelt 1995).One common form of normativism consists simply in counter-arguments to naturalism without clear endorsement of normativism (e.g., Kingma 2010).

Hybrid positions have also been held. Focusing on mental disorders, Wakefield has proposed that the two requirements of harm and biological dysfunction must both be met for a condition to truly be pathological (Wakefield 1992).

The development of these views and their criticism has fed a voluminous literature which has now reached a certain level of sophistication, sufficient to scare off many newcomers. At the same time, skepticism has grown over the possibility or utility of a definition of health or disease (Hesslow 1993; Worrall & Worrall 2001). Somewhat paradoxically, the number of articles dedicated to the question has substantially increased.

1.2 Philosophy of Medicine Is Not the Philosophy of the Sciences of Health and Disease

How and why doctors judge that you have depression and treat you is a question about practice. Practice is one thing. Among the many reasons why doctors judge and treat depression as they do, one is science itself. But science is another thing. Is science justifying practice? To answer that question, it is necessary to investigate the science of diseases itself. Perhaps it contains no scientific argument to justify that a condition is a disease. At the very least, one needs to examine this literature to answer the question. There is no other reason why recent handbooks see philosophy of medicine essentially "as part of the Anglophone philosophy of science tradition" (Solomon et al. 2017, 2).

Medical science is not one discipline, but many. The core science of health and disease is physiology. A surprising fact is that, on average, philosophy of medicine about health and disease is only superficially interested in its core science, as compared to how much philosophy of biology is interested in biology, philosophy of physics in physics, or even the rest of philosophy of medicine is, for instance, in scientific debates about causality or evidence in medicine. To get a sense of the level of engagement of philosophy of medicine with science, let us have a look at citations and references of articles in the health and disease debate. Citations are mentions *by* other articles, while references are mentions *to* other articles. A two-dimensional measure of the integration of the health and disease debate consists in counting how many citations and references are scientific (see Figure 1). For instance, "Health as a Theoretical Concept" (Boorse 1977), which is one of the top three papers cited in philosophy of science journals between 1977 and 2017, is marginal in medical science (with about fifty citations, by papers rarely cited themselves). This may sound unproblematic. After all, why should philosophers be cited by other disciplines if only philosophers truly understand what they do? In principle, this is valid. Yet in comparison, philosophers of biology, physics, or even medicine more broadly, do get more scientific attention (even if this remains modest). What may seem more problematic are the references. One third of the 110 articles about the health and disease debate used in the preparation of this Element do not cite *any* scientific article at all. Scientific references constitute less than 20 percent in two thirds of these articles. References often provide examples of diseases that could have been replaced by other examples and are not even always the standard or expected references about the disease in question.[1] As an example, Boorse's article cites mostly

---

[1] One exception to this situation is Jerome C. Wakefield's work on the definition of mental disorder, both mainly published in science journals and cited and discussed by psychiatrists.

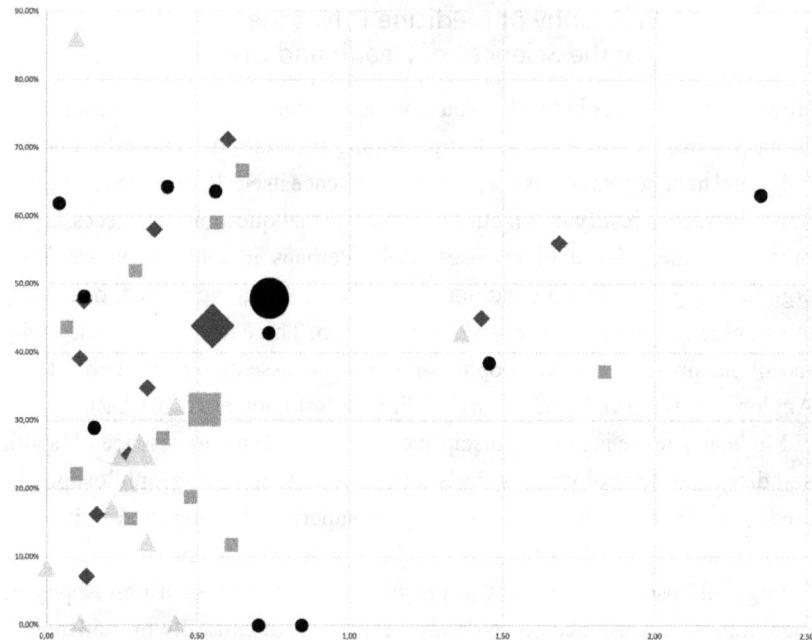

Figure 1 Bibliometric isolation of the health and disease debate from medical science, as compared to philosophy of physics relative to physics, philosophy of biology to biology and philosophy of medicine to medical science. Along the X-axis is Average Ratio of Citation (ARC) in science (Pradeu et al. 2024). An ARC of 1.00 means as many citations in a scientific field on a given year as the average article in that domain (an ARC of 0.5 means half as many and an ARC of 2.0, twice as many). Along the Y-axis is the proportion of references to science articles. Dark circles represent the 10 articles in philosophy of biology that are most cited by articles published in philosophy of science journals; light squares, in philosophy of physics; dark diamonds, in philosophy of medicine (except the health and disease debate); light triangles, in the health and disease debate. The corresponding bigger figure represents the average in each field. Philosophy of biology is the most integrated in science, the health and disease debate is the least integrated.

bibliometrically marginal articles from science journals or articles written by philosophers themselves.[2] Yet practically all of the 110 articles mentioned here cite Boorse's. This does not pose a problem for seeing how philosophy of health and disease forms a part of philosophy of medical practice. But it is very problematic for seeing how philosophy of health and disease forms a part of philosophy of science. Indeed, in contrast, philosophers of biology, physics, or

---

[2] Checked on the Web of Science on April 1, 2021.

epidemiology frequently refer to scientific sources directly, and generally cite standard or expected articles in science journals, not anecdotal or illustrative articles. Consequently, if you are interested in physiology, philosophy of medicine is not likely to be the place where you want to invest too much time (some exceptions notwithstanding).

This is, of course, a criticism of the health and disease debate in philosophy of medicine. However, one possible response is to claim that the real focus is on medical practice. In fact, some would even argue that, in the case of the health and disease debate, philosophy of medicine is not part of philosophy of science because medicine is not a science. However, not many would argue that physiology is not a science. However, many would argue, with some strong reasons, that the *basic* concepts of physiology – precisely, health and disease – are not scientific, and for that reason, there cannot be much philosophy of science in the philosophy of health and disease. If philosophy of physiology is what you are interested in, this discrepancy does not matter much. Surely, if "health" and "disease" were not scientific concepts, there would be other scientific concepts in physiology. This is the starting point for this Element. In fact, it will show that physiology offers no scientific definition of health and disease as philosophers of medicine would like it, that is, a straightforward justification that the conditions we call diseases really are diseases based on explicit and undisputable criteria. But that does not mean that physiology does not contain conceptually elaborated concepts that are crucial to the *explanation* of health and disease, and even, theories and concepts of health and disease. In fact, this is the core question: Are philosophers of medicine right in supposing that a definition of health and disease is independent from how these phenomena are described and explained, and even, that this definition must predate and predetermine our explanations of health and disease? Or is there a theoretical definition of health and disease to be found in the physiological literature?

Before we get to this key question, it is useful to get acquainted with the most influential article in philosophy of medicine: "Health as a Theoretical Concept" (Boorse 1977).

1.3 A Brief Presentation of Naturalism in Philosophy of Medicine

When I teach an introductory class on the health and disease debate, I play a little game with students. On the whiteboard, we draw both a table (just like Table 1) and a Venn diagram (just like Figure 2). I ask students to think of conditions that are or are not diseases according to them, and potential criteria that fit with all diseases and diseases only. We fill in the table and the Venn diagram at the same time in search for a correct definition.

Table 1 Possible criteria of health and disease and uncontroversial conditions of health and disease (after Boorse 1977). The corresponding numbers (E01, E02, …) are reported in Figure 2.

Criteria	Healthy conditions		Diseases
Value	E01: "mildly below average in any valuable physical quality, e.g. height, strength, endurance, coordination, reflex speed, beauty"; "regular access to food and water"	E02: Shortness; Need for sleep; blood-clotting; limb and brain regeneration; insulin production; vitamin C production; smell blindness to carbon monoxide	E03: Minor allergy or viral infection; Cowpox in smallpox epidemic; Myopia avoids infantry; Sterility in large family without contraception
Treatment by physician	E04: "circumcision, cosmetic surgery, elective abortions, and the prescription of contraceptives"; Sex change operation		
Statistical normality	E05: "normal for clinical variables like height, weight, pulse and respiration, blood pressure, vital capacity, basal metabolism, sedimentation rate"; 95 mm Hg as maximum normal diastolic blood; type O blood; red hair		E06: Dwarfism; Gigantism; atherosclerosis, minor lung inflammation; tooth decay
Pain, suffering, discomfort	E07: "teething, menstruation, and childbirth"		E08: "asymptomatic disease of many kinds-tuberculosis, diabetes, liver cirrhosis, breast cancer, various forms of heart disease, syphilis"; "a complete absence of "subjective distress" is compatible with severe internal lesions"
Disability	E09: Pregnancy; "inability to swim, fly, or see in the dark like a cat"; inability to walk in babies		E10: Death; athlete's foot, eczema, and warts; myopia and color blindness; inability to walk in adults
Adaptation	E11: Parent not becoming "healthier with each successive child"; Small stocky Durham miner; "violin playing, tightrope walking, impersonating a President"		E12: Inflammation
Homeostasis	E13: "blood temperature, acidity, speed of flow"; "composition"; perception, locomotion, growth, reproduction		E14: "deafness, limb paralysis, dwarfism, sterility"
Generic usage of "disease" (including injuries)	E16: Emmetropia ; Correct lens refraction	E15: Malaria, smallpox, cholera, tuberculosis, cancer	E17: malaria and syphilis; spina bifida; cancer; limb paralysis; injuries, causes of death; Obesity; Inanition; Seasickness; Broken bones; Gunshot wounds; foreign bodies in the stomach, supernumerary toes, animal bites, and drowning, electrocution, asphyxiation, incineration, "general crushing"

"universals or types of unhealthy conditions"		E18: "cystic fibrosis bronchial asthma, trichinosis"
Disease entity		E19: Fever, diarrhea, breathing difficulty, hypoglycemia; Acidosis, glycosuria
Intrinsic/ instrumental health	E20: Unhealthy habits, like smoking; Unhealthy environments, like New York / Vermiform appendix; High tolerance for arsenic; Mutant immunity to the common cold	E21: Appendicitis
Function	E22: peacock's tail attracts peahen, gills in fish and respiration, numerous functions of the human hypothalamus	
goal	E23: web-spinning, nest-building, or prey-catching	
individual and species survival and reproduction	E24: heart pumps blood and produces heart sounds; kidney eliminates waste and keeps bladder full	
Species design	E25: human lens focuses light on the retina; squirrel saved from a car by catching its tail in a crack; ideal types of organisms of frog, hydra, earthworm, starfish, crocodile, shark, rhesus monkey	E26: Cataract, no lens; pancreatitis requires having a pancreas that typically secretes digestive enzymes
Polymorphic functional traits / Reference class	E27: Type A, B, AB, O blood; Blue, brown, green iris; amount of skin pigmentation; either ovaries or testicles, either wombs or penises, either large or small breasts; life stages; bone growth in infant, not adult; sperm production or ovulation in adults, not infants	
Normal functioning	E28: unusual cardiovascular ability of long-distance runner	
efficiency	E29: thyroid secretes right amount of hormones; Temperature maintenance; Digestion (E29)	E30: Tuberculosis, emphysema; Cardiovascular disease; Fever, vomiting, loss of appetite

Table 1 (cont.)

Latent or asymptomatic disease	E31: Diabetes; Hepatic cirrhosis; Nephritis; Pancreatic cancer; intestinal polyp
Diseases with atypical functioning	E32: Rabies; Phenylketonuria; Herpes zoster; Vitiligo
Not life-threatening dysfunction	E33: Diseases implying melanin deficiency, deafness, diminished sense of smell
Functional readiness	E34: Not seeing with closed eyes; digestion without food; Adrenalin secretion under stress; Sweating when temperature is rising; Blood clotting after wound	E35: Hemophiliacs protected from injuries; Diabetes taking insulin daily
Risk of various diseases	E36: individual variations of body build and probability of cardiovascular disease or complications in childbirth; unusual beauty and mating success	
Extremal diseases		E37: hyperemia and anemia, hyperthyroidism and hypothyroidism, galactorrhea and agalactia; night blindness
Normal variation	E38: Normal man unable to lift a heavy weight	E39: strong man with Addison's disease unable to lift heavy weight; abnormality of microfunction, adrenocortical secretion, in Addison's disease
Structural disease		E40: congenital absence of appendix, dextrocardia, calcified pineal gland; minor deformities (nose, ear, hymen); some internal tumors; macacus ear
Universal disease		E41: benign hypertrophy of the prostate in old men

Note: Grey cells represent that Boorse does not give any explicit example.

Philosophy of Physiology

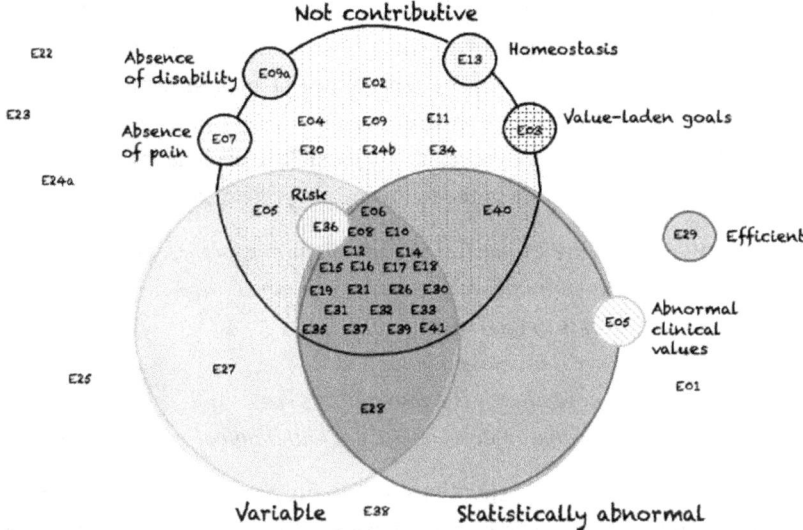

Figure 2 A Venn diagram presenting the results of the definition of "disease" in Boorse (1977). Conditions listed in Table 1 (E01, E02, etc.) are represented in extension. The central set contains diseases.

This is a rigorous reconstruction of what Boorse did many decades ago. The definition he proposed was based on a systematic confrontation of a set of forty-one types of conditions with a set of twenty-nine general candidate criteria for health and disease (Table 1). He first showed that none of the latter correctly covers all of the former (and only the former). For example, if you want to define a disease as "what a physician treats," you will run into the objection that "circumcision, cosmetic surgery, elective abortion and the prescription of contraceptives" (Boorse 1977) are medical treatments of conditions that are not diseases. Taking the time to go through this table is the best way to understand how the health and disease debate works.

Then the BST paves its way out of this morass by combining some of these criteria in a very elegant way. Recall that it defines "disease" as "a type of internal state which impairs health, *i.e.*, reduces one or more functional abilities below typical efficiency" (Boorse 1977). This definition can be reconstructed as follows. First, it relies on three basic concepts: contribution, variation, and statistical normality. A contribution is what a part of an organism may do to the survival or reproduction of the organism. A variation is the existence, in a species, of differences in the same trait and, possibly, in its contribution. Statistical normality is the fact that the most frequent values of a variable trait are concentrated into a small interval as compared to the interval of possible values, for example, that most humans in a given class have systolic blood pressure of around 12 mmHg (the pressure of the blood in the arteries during contraction as measured in millimeters of height in a standard column of mercury) while some show extreme values as low as 7 mmHg or as high as 20 mmHg. Given these three concepts, it is possible to exclude some traits from the set of diseases according to the following six principles:

(1) *no trait contributive to survival or reproduction is pathological*
(2) *some traits not contributive to survival or reproduction are not pathological*
(3) *no invariant trait is pathological*
(4) *some variable traits are not pathological*
(5) *no statistically normal trait is pathological*
(6) *some statistically abnormal traits are not pathological*

Additional, more local concepts (intrinsic health, functional readiness, polymorphic traits, asymptomatic disease, universal disease, etc.) are necessary to eliminate further subsets of cases from the set of diseases, while some of these concepts are defined by other concepts (e.g., variation by "species design" and "statistical normality" by efficiency and reference class). The results are summarized in Figure 2.

For anyone interested in how this beautiful reconstruction stands the test of counterexamples and counterarguments, the best option is to read the articles by Boorse provided in the references of this Element. Boorse also summarizes most objections and answers them. What we are interested in is why the BST is not a good basis for philosophers of physiology, in spite of its apparently scientific terms ("function," "statistical normality," "reference class," etc.) and concrete examples.

1.4 Naturalism Does Not Investigate the Science of Health and Disease

Here is a puzzling question. On the one hand, when scientists investigate a phenomenon X, they must rely on some definition of X that determines what they consider to be cases of X. On the other hand, a definition of X must rely on some knowledge of X that is obtained through investigation. There are two ways out of this circle. The first is that the phenomenon is defined a priori, that is, clearly and once and for all, by more general properties that have been investigated by broader disciplines. The second way out of the circle is that definition and investigation progress together, and that definitions are temporary and hypothetical until knowledge is stabilized. Are health and disease concepts of the first sort or of the second sort?

Most contributions to the health and disease debate endorse the first view. Philosophy of physiology starts when one embraces the second view. I call the first view *foundationalism* about health and disease, which holds that health and disease are *basic, non-empirical,* and *invariable* concepts that frame medical science and practice. Let us investigate these claims in turn.

First, health and disease are *non-empirical concepts*. This claim relies on two ideas, (1) that medical science contains fine-grained descriptions of specific diseases and the corresponding normal processes but never elaborates any encompassing conception of what a disease in general (or health) consists in, and that (2) such a *general* conception of disease is independent from these descriptions of *particular* diseases. As a consequence, the empirical details are irrelevant to a description of what disease is in general, even for a naturalist. This thus requires an elaboration of the concept of disease that is based on concepts *external* to physiology. This is indeed what normativists do, consistently, when they describe "disease" as a disvalued, or harmful state of the body (or mind) that impairs our ability to be happy, and so on. The situation is trickier for naturalists, who want both to define health and disease a priori *and* in physiological terms.

To solve this problem, Boorse has used some non-specifically physiological concepts such as "function" and "statistical normality" that are indeed used in physiology. He has also invented abstract concepts that are supposed to describe the foundations of physiology, such as "reference class" and "species design." A *reference class* is defined as a "natural class of organisms of uniform functional design," with "characters [that] occur together" (Boorse 1977), and which provides standards to establish a statistically normal level of efficiency. This term is forged by Boorse against objections such as: it is statistically normal for an adult woman, not for a man, to have ovaries – a man without functional ovaries has no disease. Yet "reference class" seems to substitute for the epidemiological concept of a population, and it has been shown not to be very useful – indeed, any class could, in principle, become a reference class, and anything be deemed normal or abnormal accordingly (Kingma 2007). A "species design" is "the typical hierarchy of interlocking functional systems that supports the life of organisms of that type" (Boorse 1977). It is therefore normal for a frog not to fly, because this is not a part of the "species design." However, if medical scientists really used such a concept, it would be biological nonsense (Ereshefsky 2009). Indeed, the *physiological description* of an organism is not committed to the existence of a "species design." Moreover, most physiological functions are shared widely across all mammals. The existence of most biological functions has even been established in small samples of organisms of the same or of different species, then extrapolated, and their "level of efficiency" is not known. The "typical hierarchy of interlocking functional systems" itself remains largely unknown. In fact, physiology simply proposes hypotheses on how things work, not norms on how they should work.

Another such abstract concept discussed by naturalists is "situation-specificity," that is, the fact that the level of a function is normal or pathological depending on the situation (or environment) of the organism. Philosophers of medicine use this concept to deflect the objection that it is normal for a poisoned digestive system not to be able to digest, or for the heart rate to be high during strenuous exercise (Hausman 2011). This concept as well may make the concept of health and disease intractable (Kingma 2010, 2016). The term seems to summarize key experimental concepts such as *factors*, *parameters*, and *exposure*. It is normal that organisms shiver when *exposed* to cold; social life is a *factor* of the normal duration of sleep, which also varies because of some individual physiological *parameters*. However, this does not mean that physiologists must establish normal values for each specific situation, but that they must explain how normal organisms adapt as a function of factors, parameters, and exposure. Physiology investigates biological functions in all their variations, that is, with the idea that there is not one normal reaction for each situation, but one normal function adapting to various degrees to various situations. Physiology thereby establishes values that likely indicate health in a limited set of defined, standard situations – not normal values for every possible situation. The idea of "situation-specific" norms is an exaggerated account inspired by the idea that medical science is all about establishing norms. In general, the reason for the introduction of such artificial terms as "reference class," "species design," and "situation-specificity" in the description of physiology, is not exactly to account for health and disease as physiology describes them. Instead, it is to defend or attack the presumed objectivity of proposed criteria of health and disease. Most of these supposedly defining concepts are ad hoc creations for that purpose.

The second claim is that health and disease are *invariable* concepts. All the recent developments of medical science are supposed to fall inside this supposedly perennial framework and simply provide further technical details. To put it bluntly, the exact same description of the naturalistic concepts of health and disease could have been given at the time of Galen, based on the descriptions of diseases in the medical science of imperial Rome. In fact, it has:

> Surely whenever there is no impediment in any of the activities of all their bodily parts, people say that they are healthy and think that they have no need of doctors; but whenever they become aware that some one of their natural functions is beginning to perform either badly or not at all, they consider themselves to be sick in that section of the body whose activity they see to be

impaired and they call upon the aid of a doctor to cure it. I see all men using the nouns "health" and "sickness" thus; and this is the conception which I claimed that everyone observes in the case of these words and furthermore in addition to them no less in the case of all nouns and verbs which are cognate with them. (Galen 1991)

Boorse explicitly roots his "Biostatistical Theory" of health and disease in this Galenic tradition, citing it favorably at the beginning of his major article (Boorse 1977). Consequently, conceptual analysis in philosophy of medicine does not require any specific, or historically updated, medical knowledge, whereas it would in philosophy of biology or philosophy of physics. All you need to know is a sufficient number of conditions with their status and, at best, main dysfunction (if any). Remember my whiteboard exercise. To play the game, you simply need to know that pregnancy is not a disease, but diabetes is, and so on, and that pregnancy consists in bearing a future child, while diabetes consists in having too much sugar in your blood. Based on that, you are simply looking for common criteria that fits with the status of these three conditions and many more, or object to your opponent's definition by simply finding a counterexample (detailed descriptions can be found in Schwartz 2007; Lemoine 2013).

This "game," as Boorse himself once called it, has been criticized for many reasons. One is that not many concepts can be defined by necessary and sufficient conditions (Schwartz 2007; Sadegh-Zadeh 2008). Another line of criticism is that conceptual analysis gives priority to folk notions of health and disease. Some have explicitly investigated the folk "models" of health and disease in medical practice (Hofmann 2005). Many more contributions in philosophy of medicine have implicitly done the same: analyze intuitions of medical doctors, rather than basic concepts of medical science. Yet, as observed by Murphy and Woolfolk, "from the point of view of the philosophical analysis of scientific terms, the scientific illiteracy of everyday intuitions is just unfortunate for lay concepts" (Murphy & Woolfolk 2000). A third line of criticism is that conceptual analysis cannot rule out artificial definitions or decide between conflicting definitions that fit with the accepted examples (Lemoine 2013). Plato has famously proposed the definition of a "man" as a "featherless biped." Conceptual analysis may lead to such artificial definitions simply because there is no rule that imposes the usage of terms of the art. A last line of criticism is that it is, in fact, impossible to determine whether a condition is a disease or not independently from the knowledge of this disease. For instance, atherosclerosis is traditionally defined as "a condition in which an artery wall thickens as a result of the accumulation of fatty materials such as cholesterol" (ICD-11). This makes it problematic as a bona fide case of disease because it is structural, universal, progressive with age, and comes in degrees of severity (Boorse 1977). Yet, since the 1980s, dramatic redefinition of these conditions has focused less on occlusion by fat deposit, atheroma, and structural degradation, and focused instead on homeostatic functions of the endothelium related to vasoconstriction (e.g., Deanfield et al. 2007). Some have proposed the hypothesis that an equilibrium, described as the homeostatic endothelium, is disrupted, and replaced by a noxious feedback process. Not every thickening of the artery is pathological in this view and this affects how you classify the condition, which in turn affects the exact boundaries of the class. Finally, this may also affect the criteria of your definition. If all this is true, boundaries cannot be invariable, and a definition must take into account scientific knowledge of those conditions.

The third claim of foundationalism is that health and disease are *basic* concepts for medical science. This means that they are not established *inductively*, that is, by generalization from *facts* that medical science progressively discovers about diseases. Instead, these concepts can only be clarified by *deduction* from even more general concepts, and more specific diseases should be established as such by deduction from the broad concept of disease. The apparently "inductive" approach Boorse (and others) adopt consists only in checking whether the general features of "health" and disease" they hypothesize a priori indeed fit with the various conditions medical science defines as diseases – is condition X "dysfunctional," "statistically abnormal," "maladaptive," "harmful," and so on. Instead, a truly inductive approach would admit that "health" and "disease" are not defined once and for all and that they depend on the discovery of various mechanisms at play in the pathophysiology of various diseases. A philosopher endorsing this inductive approach would consider these mechanisms as the true content of the concept of disease, and the description of the physiology of the body as containing the mechanisms that should define "health." For instance, if we found that in nine cases out of ten, diseases are caused by a recently discovered process that is rarely present in what we call healthy conditions – say, inflammation – this would not change the definition of "disease" according to foundationalism. While medical researchers may consider this a theory of disease, from which a powerful definition of disease follows, and may consider non-inflammatory conditions to be defined differently, foundationalism would simply see this as a theory of how *some* diseases work. Indeed, the foundationalist concept of disease cannot be changed. It can simply be properly analyzed, that is, derived from broader concepts such as "incapacity," "harm," "typical," and "situation." The function of this concept is to justify that a medical theory really is a theory of a disease, and the foundationalist credo is that nothing else can, so that without such a basic concept, anything would count as a disease if doctors, or pharmaceutical companies, so decided.

Yet, medical researchers typically use an inductive strategy to establish whether a controversial condition is, or is not, a disease. In a controversial condition, they look for material, generic processes that underlie other known diseases, and for specific variations in the process that explains this disease only. Typically, schizophrenia has been hypothesized to be a specific form of homeostatic dysregulation of dopamine, or a fetal infection by *Toxoplasma gondii*, or a genetically predisposed deficiency in the treatment of information by the brain. In any of these options, schizophrenia would belong to a set of uncontroversial diseases. A foundationalist would object that such processes as "infection" must be established as pathological in the first place. For medical scientists, however, a process is preliminarily *hypothesized* as pathological because it explains statistically abnormal levels of efficiency or harmful conditions – or for any vague and general feature generally found in diseases. That would be the case for infection. However, once it is sufficiently documented in accepted pathological conditions, that is, precisely and specifically, it serves as sufficient evidence in itself that any new condition that involves it is actually a disease, *even if* it is not statistically abnormal or harmful. On the contrary, as long as no explanation can be found in terms of infection, for example, a condition will remain controversial.

Why is naturalism so far away from physiology? The reason is that it has never evolved from a polemic question of the 1970s into a single field of investigation. Although naturalism confronts normativism with the claim that having a disease essentially relies on the existence of biological dysfunction rather than on a value judgment, naturalism is still, essentially, about the role of values in medical practice. For Boorse, the raison d'être of "naturalism" is to establish that disease is "a value-free concept," not to establish with exactness what we know about the biological fact of disease (see Lemoine & Giroux 2016). This question about practice is still pervasive and seems to frame the health and disease debate. In comparison, philosophers of biology *may* have practical goals (like opposing creationism or criticizing the moral consequences of essentialism), but their legitimacy in doing that as philosophers of science *necessarily* relies on the pursuit of a theoretical goal, that is, clarifying scientific concepts as they are used in contemporary science. In the health and disease debate, the practical goal is explicit in 62 of the 110 articles mentioned earlier. A total of 79 articles out of 110 explicitly take a side, naturalism, or normativism, and 47 of them develop anti-naturalistic arguments without necessarily endorsing normativism explicitly. In other terms, philosophers of medicine, including naturalists, are interested in discussing the justification for medical judgments rather than in examining the nature of the phenomena of health and disease. This is legitimate if the goal is to discuss the implications of having concepts of health and disease. But this is at odds with discussing related concepts within the medical sciences.

1.5 The Idea of a Philosophy of Physiology

Medical researchers investigate fascinating *processes* such as infection and inflammation mentioned earlier, but also dysbiosis, auto-immunity, neoplasm, proteopathy, endothelial dysfunction, decompensation, homeostasis, maintenance, repair, regeneration, and so on, and *properties* such as virulence and pathogenicity, penetrance, genotoxicity, teratogenicity, and resilience. In this Element, I will present some of those processes and properties. They explain what is happening in the many diseases we all know or have heard of. They together constitute the field of the pathological phenomenon – the natural phenomenon of disease, as it exists on our planet in all its diversity. They also raise many conceptual difficulties. This is the field that us philosophers of physiology want to investigate. We are interested in conceptual questions about how disease, but also health, are explained. We think that if there is any scientific definition of health and disease, it is to be found in how they are explained.

As a guide to this vast field, we will follow the thread of a question: is there a theory of disease and a science of health in physiology? In medicine, it is true that no theoretical part of medicine discusses "health" and "disease" the way theoretical biology discusses "organism," "function," "metabolism," or the origin of life (Hesslow 1993). However, it is indeed "health" and "disease" that are indirectly elaborated through more technical and seemingly local concepts. These discussions have consequences for the empirical content of theories. They are necessary to understand physiological science and they organize a body of knowledge. They are used in biomedical theories and they are necessary to identify theoretically important problems. They do everything the concepts of health and disease, themselves, according to Hesslow, do not. In fact, a mistake of skepticism is to conclude that they do not play a major role in medical science because they do not play the role of *foundational concepts*. The fact is that the concepts of "health" and "disease" are progressively defined, in medical science, by induction and recursion, through a set of more precise and specific concepts. In this Element, we will call these more precise and specific concepts – inflammation, infection, dysbiosis, pathogenicity, neoplasm, and so on – *disease-related concepts*.

I will try to convince you that the search for a theory that explains health and disease is a constant preoccupation of medical researchers. Far from neglecting this question and leaving it aside for philosophers to deal with, they are much more aware of how difficult the question is. In their collective quest for an answer, they are progressively *naturalizing* the concepts of health and disease, that is, they are transforming two terms that originate in commonsense, are vaguely defined or even rigorously redefined by philosophers, into a precise, technical, operational, and scientifically useful set of concepts based in natural science (Lemoine 2014). They are not "presupposing" any preliminary definition in any strong sense of "presupposing." They are certainly leaning on intuitions, but it is not to justify these intuitions by scientific theories; indeed, they are very likely to go beyond these intuitions or prove them wrong. A handful of philosophers of medicine have endorsed this description of naturalization in the health and disease debate (Griffiths & Matthewson 2016; Fuller 2018; Sholl 2020; Sholl & Okholm 2021). If I fail to convince you that physiology is building a theory of health and disease, I hope to have at least convinced you that this field is full of interesting conceptual issues for philosophers of science to investigate.

In short, the goal of the present section was to show how futile it may be to investigate *definitions* of health and disease without any consideration for how they are *explained* in medical science. The rest of this Element investigates these disease-related concepts at various levels of generality called "disease entities," "theories of diseases" (in the plural) and, finally, "theories of disease" (in the singular), and the science of health.

2 Disease Entities and Pathophysiological Processes

There are 17,000 diseases in the last version of the International Classification of Diseases (ICD-11). A typically philosophical question is: what do they have in common, if anything? Commonsense would propose a set of intuitive answers: they are unpleasant, incapacitating, dysfunctional, or harmful. Is that all there is to diseases?

Let us investigate one of them. Diabetes mellitus is a disease, a recognizable condition diagnosed in many human patients. To diagnose a condition, doctors must know typical signs and symptoms of that condition and, on this basis, distinguish it from conditions it closely resembles. Symptoms are often defined as reported, or experienced, by the patient (e.g., pain, fever, swelling, incapacity to walk), while signs are often defined as found by the doctor through an investigation of some sort (e.g., high blood pressure, high sugar level in the blood, abnormal spot in X-ray imagery, subtly abnormal motor control of hands). To predict and treat a condition, doctors also need to know its causes and how it works. For instance, diabetes mellitus type 2 (T2D) is, most often, a late-life and progressive condition of chronically high blood glucose (and other signs), caused by diet and lifestyle and, to some extent, reversible by strict change in diet and lifestyle, while diabetes mellitus type 1 (T1D) is, generally, an early-life condition of chronically high blood glucose (and other signs), with more sudden onset, caused by irreversible, autoimmune destruction of beta cells in the pancreas. What any diseases have in common must be causes, process, or manifestations.

The diagnostic science of diseases is called "semiology," that is, the "science of the signs" of diseases. There is also a biological science of the processes of diseases, called "pathophysiology." The *process* itself is also called the pathophysiology of, say, T2D. What doctors call a "disease entity" is a specific form of pathological phenomenon ideally characterized both by specific signs and by a specific pathophysiology – present in all patients with that disease. However, semiology and pathophysiology of a disease are rarely specific. Many signs can be observed in many diseases. Many pathophysiological processes enter in the pathophysiology of many diseases. Surely, some are exclusive. For instance, "insulin resistance," the progressive unresponsiveness of cell receptors to insulin, when chronic, is a pathophysiological process supposed to be specific to T2D. It causes hyperglycemia and exhausts insulin secretion, which are two pathophysiological processes known to be shared with T1D. Another component of both types of diabetes mellitus is chronic inflammation, a pathophysiological process also common to many other disease entities. In fact, if many pathophysiological processes participate in the pathophysiology of many diseases, a disease entity is characterized by a *specific* nexus of pathophysiological processes. For that reason, pathophysiology can either be conceived as the science of distinct and separate disease entities, or as the science of pathophysiological processes interacting with one another in many ways. These distinct views are not opposed. However, they provide different perspectives on "the pathological phenomenon": on the one hand, there are thousands of typical abnormal conditions with many shared properties but none in common with all, apart from trivial features like "incapacitating," "dysfunctional," or "harmful," and the more we get fixed on specific disease entities, the more precise the diagnosis; on the other hand, there are at most a few dozen common pathophysiological processes, caused by, or causing, more specific processes, and the fewer there are, the simpler the explanation. In the latter perhaps lies a unitary view of disease.

2.1 Robust Disease Entities Rely on the Description of Specific Pathophysiological Processes

In *Harrison's Principles of Internal Medicine*,[3] there is one description for both diabetes mellitus types 1 and 2. It is divided up into classification, epidemiology, diagnosis, "regulation of glucose homeostasis," pathogenesis, and the presentation of some monogenic forms of diabetes mellitus. However, there is no canonical way the knowledge about a disease entity is supposed to be

---

[3] https://accessmedicine.mhmedical.com/book.aspx?bookid=2129 (last access on May 27, 2021).

organized. In the same handbook, the descriptions of breast cancer and influenza are organized differently. That said, an analytic definition of "disease entity" can be:

the description of a specific disease type that consists in:

(1) **pathogeny**, that is the process where a set of causes external to the disease itself triggers it (these causes are called the "**etiology** of the disease"),
(2) the various mechanisms composing the process of the disease itself (**pathophysiology**),
(3) signs and symptoms (**pathology** and **semiology**), including
   a. alternative combinations of signs and symptoms that sometimes manifest in different ways (**clinical forms**),
   b. characteristic courses (**natural history**), for example, initial rash peaking with a high fever and improving until complete remission, leaving scars,
   c. a set of explicit, sufficient differences from other disease entities (**differential diagnosis**),
   d. the capacity to clearly group a certain set of individual cases (**nosology**),
(4) the ability to explain why and how the disease happens in relation to why and how it can, or cannot, be treated, and with what expected effects (**therapeutics**, including **prevention**).[4]

The main goal of disease entities is to organize knowledge. Most studies in medical science, whether they are investigating the pathophysiology of a disease, the sensitivity and specificity of a diagnostic test, or the efficiency of a treatment, are generally led in groups of patients that share the same disease entity. Although doctors may treat patients even when they cannot fit their state with any disease entity, the reliability, safety, and scientific nature of medicine depends upon disease entities. Consequently, a crucial task for science is to correctly distinguish different disease entities. The International Classification of Diseases summarizes official disease entities. It provides a short description of the specificity of the disease, an explicit but stipulated inclusion of various forms of the disease and exclusions of other disease entities, and possible pathological manifestations. See Table 2 for an example.

The key feature of any nosological system, that is, a list of disease entities, is the distinctions it allows to make between these disease entities. The distinctions can be designed to optimize many properties of such a system, as philosophers of medicine have pointed out, including observational fidelity, explanatory power, predictive power, or correspondence to available treatments

---

[4] A simpler version of this template is proposed in Thagard (1999). See also Whitbeck (1977).

Table 2 The ICD description of "Diabetes mellitus type 2" (consulted on May 26th, 2021).

Description

Diabetes mellitus type 2 (formerly noninsulin-dependent diabetes mellitus (NIDDM) or adult-onset diabetes) is a metabolic disorder that is characterized by high blood glucose in the context of insulin resistance and relative insulin deficiency.

Inclusions
- non-insulin-dependent diabetes of the young

Exclusions
- Diabetes mellitus in pregnancy (JA63)
- Diabetes mellitus, other specified type (5A13)
- Idiopathic Type 1 diabetes mellitus (5A10)

Coded Elsewhere
- Pre-existing type 2 diabetes mellitus in pregnancy (JA63.1)

Has manifestations
- Acute complications of diabetes mellitus
- 5A44 Insulin-resistance syndromes
- 8C03.0 Diabetic polyneuropathy
- Mononeuropathy
- 8D88.1 Autonomic neuropathy due to diabetes mellitus
- 9B10.21 Diabetic cataract
- 9B71.0 Diabetic retinopathy
- 11 Diseases of the circulatory system
- 13 Diseases of the digestive system
- EB90.0 Diabetic skin lesions
- 15 Diseases of the musculoskeletal system or connective tissue
- FA38.0 Diabetic arthropathy
- FA38.1 Neuropathic arthropathy
- 16 Diseases of the genitourinary system
- GB61 Chronic kidney disease
- MC85 Gangrene"

(Tsou 2012; Tabb 2015, 2020; Keuck & Hauswald 2016). Another requirement for any good nosological system is that they respect two principles stated by Hucklenbroich (2014):

(1) "Principle of completeness": Every case of disease is a case of a specific disease. An unspecified case of disease is either an unknown case of a disease, or a case of an unknown disease.

(2) "Principle of unambiguousness": Every case of a disease is a case of one disease only. Patients may nevertheless be affected by two diseases at the same time.

Which of the necessary components of a disease entity justifies that a set of pathological manifestations be grouped into a specific disease entity? Some philosophers have proposed original views on this question,[5] but the scientific consensus is rather that specificity relies on pathophysiology. There are, in fact, relatively few symptoms of disease, and few sets of symptoms that are specific to a given disease. For that reason, diagnosis relies more solidly on specific signs. The specificity of signs increases with their centrality in the pathophysiological process. Signs of systemic inflammation (e.g., in the blood) are not very specific to any condition, while signs of local inflammation (a red, swollen, hot protuberance under the skin) are more specific, and the detected presence of a certain toxin on the inflammatory spot is perfectly specific. Thus, the pathophysiology of a disease entity justifies that it is considered as a specific disease entity. When it turns out to be the same in two disease entities, they merge into one with different clinical forms. When it turns out to be different in two clinical forms, they are defined as separate disease entities. These questions are related to the debate between "lumpers" and "splitters" in psychiatry (Craver 2009) or elsewhere.

A good test of how important pathophysiological processes are is to consider how some areas of medicine are doing without solid knowledge of these processes. Psychiatry, as a matter of fact, does not offer disease entities robustly based on known pathophysiological processes. As a result, its nosological system is subjected to more controversies than other fields of medicine. Some of the conditions it diagnoses as pathological are controversial because of the very relevance of seeing them as such (see the historical controversy about homosexuality), others, because of the criteria that are used to diagnose them (e.g., how do psychiatrists diagnose a "major depressive episode"?). That said, it is interesting to see how researchers have tried to bypass pathophysiological processes to build nosological systems anyway. These debates revolve around the notion of a "crisp" diagnosis, that is, one that distinguishes who has disease X from who does not. The opposite of a crisp diagnosis is a fuzzy diagnosis, that is, a diagnosis that cannot always tell with certainty that you have disease X or not. To improve crispness, researchers may try to improve 5 properties of their proposed diagnostic criteria:

---

[5] Philosophers have defended original versions of the specificity of disease entities based on etiology (Whitbeck 1977), natural history (Hucklenbroich 2014), or "reasonable applicability" and "reasonable predictability" (Severinsen 2001) of the manifestation-specificity of disease entities.

- *Operationality*: explicit, person-independent, verifiable nature of a criterion to reduce vagueness, that is, observable ambiguities and relative inapplicability, with a tradeoff between reliability and validity (Millon et al. 2010, 175), as well as a risk that the early operationalization of a concept leads to diagnostic rigidity (Maj and Gaebel 2002, 21; Millon et al. 2010, 178–179). This is just to avoid divergence between doctors that would add to the divergence between criteria and factual differences in pathophysiology (if any exist, that is).
- *Theory-independence*: atheoretical, neutral criteria (American Psychiatric Association 2000, xvii–xviii), in particular, "with regard to etiology" (American Psychiatric Association 1987, xxiv). On the contrary, when the physiopathology is correctly hypothesized, a theory-dependent criterion is obviously much better.
- *Categorical* or *dimensional*: determining membership according to binary properties (e.g., present/absent), or thresholds in quantitative values (Kendell and Jablensky 2003; Cooper 2007, 53). If a pathophysiological process is known, it is also known whether the process is pathological when the outcome is quantitatively out of range (e.g., blood pressure), or when the process does not take place in a healthy body at all (e.g., viral infection). When the pathophysiology is unknown, this choice comes down to a best guess.
- *Monothetic* or *polythetic*: necessary (and jointly sufficient) for a situation to qualify as a case or determining alternative sets of criteria. Polythetic concepts are liable for a greater heterogeneity of the delimited class, and increase the risk of false positive cases (Helzer et al. 2008, 21), but may be a necessary evil in the face of individual variation (Millon et al. 2010, 89). This is a clever way to deal with diagnosis when pathophysiology is unknown. When it is known, it is most often not necessary.
- *Prototypicity*: a set of highly characteristic features, or an individual characteristic case, or series of cases, with a degree of closeness or resemblance that defines membership to the class (see Westen's section in Millon et al. 2010). Prototype approaches are probably a better match with how the clinician naturally diagnoses, but do not necessarily produce crisper diagnostic sets. They reflect how doctors spontaneously categorize abnormal conditions, but not necessarily the underlying abnormal pathophysiology.

Disease entities have mostly been controversial where pathophysiological knowledge is insufficient. Alternative formal approaches to disease entities have generally been proposed to make for insufficient knowledge, without much result. Overmedicalization has prompted reflection on the need for sophisticated thresholds for diagnostic and therapeutic decisions, while debates between lumpers and splitters have fueled the usage of statistical tools and fuzzy logic.

This is enough to show how crucial the knowledge of pathophysiology is to medical science and how distinct this is from the terms of the health and disease debate.

2.2 The Pathological Phenomenon Consists in a Small Number of Pathophysiological Processes

If pathophysiology unifies each disease entity, does anything unify the pathophysiology of *all* disease entities? Obviously, the concept of disease does, at least in a trivial way. We have seen that philosophy of medicine has traditionally answered that question with the presupposition that disease is some sort of a priori notion imposed on medical science. Let us investigate deeper into this question. For example, when you go to the doctor with some pathological condition, you can be in one of two situations. First, you, and possibly the doctor, acknowledge that you are *sick*, which means that you present some of the few well-known, unspecific signs and symptoms of disease (pain, fatigue, weakness, nausea, fever, rash, swelling, etc.). The doctor may at the same time not know which disease to diagnose, and simply acknowledge that something is going wrong. They may even treat the sickness without a diagnosis – for instance, prescribe an anti-inflammatory drug to alleviate the symptoms and hope they simply go away soon enough. Second, the doctor may diagnose *disease* X, that is, conclude that the corresponding pathophysiological process is developing in your organism. In this situation, you may not even *feel* sick.

Philosophers have traditionally distinguished between "illness" – which is what you mostly have in the first situation – and "disease" – which is what you have in the second situation. Generally, this is interpreted as a distinction between the subjective and objective, or values and facts, or commonsense and science (Boorse 1975). On the one hand, the unity of the concept of disease is defined by what is common to illnesses – for example, the experience of harm. On the other hand, it is defined by what is common to all disease entities, for example, that they involve some form of dysfunction. Here, we are stuck in the debate between normativists and naturalists mentioned in the previous section. In light of the previous subsection, the difference between "being *sick*" and "having a *disease*" can be more precisely interpreted as a difference between manifestations and their underlying processes, description, and explanation. From a scientific point of view, unifying the field of the pathological by its manifestations makes less sense than unifying by its explanations. As seen in the previous section, naturalism has failed to consider this possibility because it has presupposed that the concept of disease should somehow be a priori, and that the specific diseases are diseases only because they match the criteria of disease in general.

A useful phrase to introduce at this stage is "the pathological phenomenon," to refer to all the pathological phenomena collectively. The pathological phenomenon is not a concept with an extension to possible or conceivable conditions – as if we had a definition that could work with any possible disease in any possible organism living in any possible world. Instead, it is a fact as we observe it in organisms in this world, even if we do not conceptualize it clearly. This fact is biologically important as a collective fact. There are diseases. What there is to disease is not one and the same thing, such as "diseasehood" (Sadegh-Zadeh 2008), that is supposed to be instantiated in each disease entity. Instead, it is a fact of life as we know it. All living organisms are vulnerable to disease. This collective term, "the pathological phenomenon," refers to a fact that scientists sometimes study collectively, without any reference to the subdivision into many disease entities. For instance, epidemiology refers to "morbidity" or to the "burden of disease" when addressing all or many diseases at the same time. Recently, some have proposed the concept of the "diseasome" to refer to all the interactions between genes involved in all diseases (Loscalzo et al. 2007). As they grow old, many human beings suffer from multimorbidity, that is, the conjunction of several chronic diseases.

The starting point for the philosophical problem of the unity of the science of disease should be that "disease" is de facto *defined* by: "$disease_1$ or $disease_2$ or ... $disease_n$," and that these diseases are defined by the concrete description of the processes that underlie them, rather than by abstract and trivial criteria. Indeed, "disease" refers to the pathological phenomenon, which consists in the gigantic disjunctive domain of all specific diseases. It is important to start with that simple idea, even if just to acknowledge that there are too many diseases for any scientifically meaningful unifying conception to be immediately obvious. Disease is a fact before it is a unified notion.

For the pathological phenomenon to be conceived and defined, the disjunction must be reduced as much as possible (but not necessarily to one category). However, a focus on explanation seems to lead to the self-defeating consequence that there is no meaningful concept of disease for the science of diseases, only a huge list of heterogeneous conditions that may have nothing to do with one another – and this would not prevent doctors from doing a good job after all. That said, the focus on pathophysiological *processes* that explain specific diseases allows for an important reduction in the number of criteria necessary for this otherwise intractable disjunction. In other terms, if the pathological phenomenon is to be theorized and "disease" to be defined meaningfully, it has somehow to be as a disjunction of pathophysiological processes: "process$_1$ or process$_2$ or ... process$_m$," instead of a disjunction of disease entities: "disease$_1$ or disease$_2$ or ... disease$_n$," given that there are many fewer processes than entities ($m \ll n$).

Note that this reduction is already at play in the broader categories used in classifications of disease entities. For instance, a set of patients suffer from T2D, T2D is one of the forms of diabetes, diabetes is a metabolic disease, a metabolic disease is a somatic disease, and somatic disease is one of the two forms of disease (along with mental disorders). At each step, the problem is to model a type of process that explains all diseases in the group, not simply find common features that may be accidental or simply appear to be the most common to all other diseases. For instance, in the face of the description of T2D, it will not explain much about the disease to focus on trivial features such as "dysfunction" or "harm." Instead, the question is how the description of T2D participates in a hypothesized set of diseases so that a common process is revealed, which would not have been apparent otherwise. For instance, T1D and T2D involve similar disruptions in the regulation of glycemia. Grouping them reveals how T2D can evolve toward insulin dependence. Then grouping diabetes with other metabolic diseases like hyperlipidemia reveals their relation to a common higher regulatory system, its various vulnerabilities, and how different metabolic diseases may interact (e.g., in the so-called "metabolic syndrome"). Thus, the primary problem with generalization is not counterexamples, as is the case for conceptual analysis, but sterile or misleading hypotheses about types of disease. As hypotheses are many, the insight they provide consequently comes in various forms and degrees. A choice between explanatory models need not be made until everything that is explained in one is also in the other. In ICD-11, "type 2 diabetes mellitus" is currently categorized as an *endocrine* disease but described as a *metabolic* disease without much explanation. Obviously, it is both. It is also a *nutritional* disease in many cases. Each of these conceptualizations casts a different light on the disease. The problem is empirical, but also entrenched in important conceptual questions – what process characterizes all endocrine diseases? Metabolic diseases? Nutritional diseases? How should they be modeled and defined, and what should they include?

Indeed, nosology is not like the periodic table of elements, that is, final, give or take a handful of newly discovered elements. Yet, the formal structure of nosology remains relatively stable. What is constantly changing, however, are the descriptions of processes, how they explain a disease, and the types of diseases they justify. The extension of a disease changes, sometimes with philosophical, ethical, economic, and social considerations, always with a change in the description of processes. For instance, "insulin resistance" was once a description of a process specific to diabetes (Matthews et al. 1985). However, research deals with questions such as: Is "insulin resistance" an accurate or sufficient description (Goel 2015)? What is an accurate description of "insulin resistance" and does it happen in all patients with diabetes and only them (Bugianesi et al. 2005)? Only in the context of such discussions about a disease entity can other considerations be relevant in contemporary medicine.

From the point of view of the processes they share or not, diseases are grouped in tree-shape nosological structures. It is unlikely, but possible, that some groups of diseases are entirely distinct from the rest, that is, share no common process with any other disease. This may be the case for mental disorders. If it were the case, the science of such a separate group of diseases would be entirely independent.

It seems safe to hypothesize, on the contrary, that all diseases share common processes with other diseases. On the further hypothesis that these processes causally interact with one another, individual diseases can be described as the many specific manifestations of a network of pathological processes. This network can consist in a handful of major nodes and belts of minor ones, with a thicket of edges – one specific disease consisting in one of the many pathways in the network (Figure 3). Another possibility is that the network has the strong hierarchical structure of a tree with all specific diseases branching out of the same trunk through further ramifications. This is what a successful "theory of

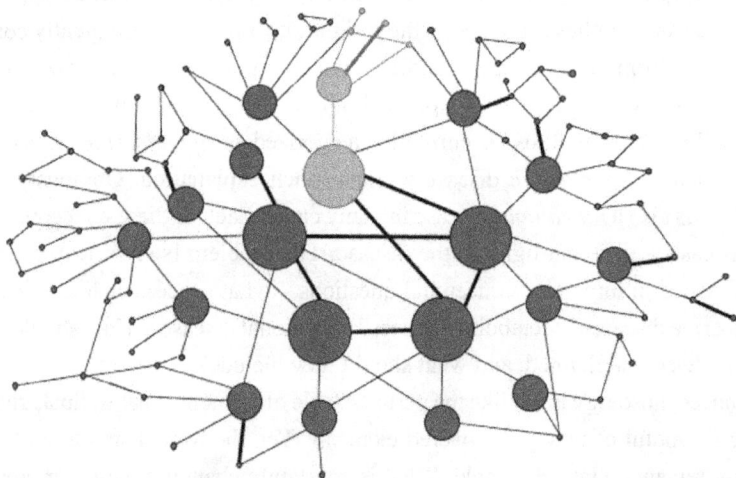

Figure 3 The pathological phenomenon as a bush of pathological processes. The more frequent a process, the bigger the node, and the more frequent the association between two processes, the thicker the edge. In lighter grey, we approach one disease.

disease" could ultimately discover (see Section 3). Whatever the situation, all diseases together do not simply form a class of phenomena with similar properties. Instead, they form one "pathological phenomenon" with infinitely many variations and manifestations in individuals. This concrete fact is what pathophysiology is keen to theorize.

In this section, we have uncovered the object of pathophysiology, namely, the "pathological phenomenon." We now want to know whether it simply consists in the juxtaposed knowledge of all the many diseases and underlying processes we have observed, or whether it can be unified into one theory – or whatever we want to call it.

3 How Generalizable Are Disease Theories?

When you are sick, you expect the doctor to diagnose a specific disease entity among thousands of possibilities. However, entire sets of these possible diseases have a lot in common. To describe a crucial process shared by a set of diseases, physiology resorts to a specific form of theories – *disease theories*. For instance, there are many infectious diseases – malaria, the flu, tuberculosis, syphilis, AIDS, to cite only a few – but a theory of infectious diseases is intended to describe the core process they all share and its many variations. Such disease theories have important functions in physiology as well as in medical science.

A first function is to provide the right description of a causal process. It should be generalizable, that is, it expands our knowledge of some specific diseases by analogy and is in contrast with what is known in other specific diseases of the same type. One common process to all infectious diseases is proliferation of a micro-organism (the "agent") in a "host organism" (e.g., the lung, the brain, the skin or the immune system of humans, or mammals, or specific species), triggering some form and degree of defense in the host, with the whole process explaining "virulence," that is, the sum of pathological effects caused in an organism or population. Since we know that, in a specific disease, the virus that causes it cannot enter a human cell and replicate in its nucleus without a specific receptor, this suggests both how other viral infections may occur and how they may differ. In other words, a disease theory illuminates the key parameters that diseases share or not, explaining both their specificities and commonalities, why they can cause disease (pathogenicity), and have such and such effects to a given degree (virulence). In so doing, such a theory establishes the boundaries of a disease type. The discovery of *Helicobacter pylori*, an agent that can settle in the stomach and cause damage in its tissue, transformed peptic ulcer from a psychosomatic into an infectious disease (Thagard 1999).

A second function is to establish that a condition is indeed a disease, if it proves to be undergirded by a typical pathological process and is explained by a disease theory. In Section 2, we mentioned the existence of an infectious theory of schizophrenia. While schizophrenia has long been somewhat controversial, evidence that it is specifically caused by an infectious agent would have been considered evidence that it is a disease. Another somewhat controversial condition is fibromyalgia. Fibromyalgia is defined as a form of widespread pain in muscles and joints that is not explained yet by any specific known factor. Some think that it is a rheumatic, autoimmune disease, others, that it is psychogenic – that is, the expression of a mental disorder – and others even think that it is just a way to express human distress (e.g., extreme fatigue or demotivation), which is not particularly pathological. However, most skeptics would be forced to capitulate if a specific virus was shown to be active in most people suffering from fibromyalgia, and almost only in them.

A third important function is for a disease theory to actively expand into a "theory of disease." By *theory of disease*, I mean a construction that describes, explains, and predicts *all* diseases by a specific pathological process. A theory of disease is a disease theory that works for all diseases – for instance, expanding the infectious theory of diseases to claim that all diseases are caused by some infection. Such a theory of disease, if it existed, would unify the field of pathophysiology in a very strong sense, even if it did not work for a few diseases. It would describe the "pathological phenomenon," as it is called in the previous section, in its entirety. A definition of "disease" would follow that would be based on what scientists know of disease, not on what folk representations are. Even if this extreme possibility is unlikely, it is nevertheless an important feature of disease theories that they keep expanding until they reach the limits of their generalizability, which could attain universality.

In this section, we will focus on the first and third functions of disease theories in turn, introducing nine disease theories that have been proposed in pathophysiology, and then discussing how a disease theory can be generalized into a theory of disease.

3.1 How Disease Theories Differ in Explaining a Disease

Disease theories describe, explain, predict, and support therapeutic intervention on pathophysiological processes more or less specifically involved in some diseases.[6] Note that diseases are sometimes grouped after a common property that is not, properly speaking, a process: for example, mental disorders,

---

[6] A pioneering epistemological work on the particular structure of these theories in medical science can be found in Schaffner (1986); see also Sadegh-Zadeh (1999, 2012).

Philosophy of Physiology 29

Table 3 Nine disease theories. The theory is given a name (in bold). Note that alternative names always exist. In italics, technical terms describe the core process that is the object of the theory.

- In the formal sense, the **homeostasis theory of disease** describes disease as the disruption of a *mechanism* with a *role* or *function* of *active regulation* or *maintenance* of a broader *system* of parts with functions or roles, through *signaling*, *control*, and *mediation*, in the face of *stress* and with a margin of *tolerance* (see Section 5.2 for more).
- According to the **infectious theory of disease**, a disease is the colonization by a *pathogen* of a host that generally mounts up a *response* of the form of a *defense*, involving a nonnull degree of *virulence*.
- The **genetic theory of disease** distinguishes two cases of genetic disease. In a strong sense, a genetic disease is a (generally rare) *Mendelian disease* that only a defined *mutation* can cause by compromising a specific step in a determined *pathway* and producing a recognizable *phenotype*. In a weak sense, a genetic disease is a (often frequent) *complex* (Botstein & Risch 2003) disease, the *risk* of which is increased by an indefinite number of undetermined genes, possibly in an undetermined way.
- The **stress theory of disease** is that *psychosocial stressors* during childhood or adulthood (*trauma*) trigger a mechanism of *vulnerability* (*diathesis*) mediated by *neuroendocrine* or *neuroimmunological* loops, which accumulate a deleterious factor, sometimes called *allostatic overload*, and which is responsible in turn for an increased risk of many diseases – defined as the effects of this same cause.
- In the **immunological theory of disease**, an immune disease is defined as a process of either *immunodeficiency* or *autoimmunity* or excessive response, often (but not always) associated with *inflammation*, as observed in the *innate* and/or *adaptive immune system* of the *host*.
- The **microbiota theory of disease** originates diseases in *dysbiosis*, which is generally defined either as the presence of a *keystone pathogen* (Hajishengallis et al. 2012) that causes an *imbalance* in the *composition* of the *microbiota* as assessed by its *metagenome*, or as an imbalance of undetermined cause, which is either the cause of, or associated with, a specific disease. Alternative versions of the theory avoid the term "dysbiosis" (Olesen & Alm 2016).
- The **theory of the developmental origin of health and disease (DOHaD)** proposes that early *exposure* during *development* tracks individual organisms into a given *phenotype* that explains their (low or high) *susceptibility* to various diseases through *phenotypic plasticity*.
- The **geroscience theory of disease** sees the accumulation of *unrepaired damage* as the main common cause of all forms of *structural decay, functional decline*, and increased incidence of disease and risk of death with age. It not only applies to the diseases of the aged, but also proposes to see forms of

Table 3 (cont.)

---

accelerated aging in diseases of the young and does not consider aging at the level of the organism only, but also at lower levels.
- The **evolutionary theory of disease** investigates why disease exists to clarify how diseases work, more specifically, how *fitness* is compatible with an imperfect degree of health. It proposes *environmental mismatch, antagonistic pleiotropy, arms races,* and *life history tradeoffs* as important explanatory concepts for all diseases.

---

neurological disorders, and skin diseases. In this case, there is no object for a disease theory.

Table 3 proposes a list of 9 disease theories of broad scope. Although they are ubiquitous in medicine, there is no article or textbook to list them as such. Sometimes, some of them are presented in an article as concurrent or complementary theories of the same disease. For that reason, the list is open to discussion, and intended only to provide an idea of the scope of concepts and theories yet to be explored by philosophers of physiology.

When confronted with a disease, scientists have a choice between these various theories (and certainly others) to determine which explains the disease better. Take T2D again. It fits with the theory of disrupted homeostasis (of glucose availability) and has traditionally been thus conceived – Cannon developed the example of the regulation of glycemia (i.e., level of glucose in the blood) in his article on homeostasis, and also mentions diabetes (Cannon 1929). It is still common to think of diabetes as the following process: glycemia cannot be maintained within the margins of tolerance of normality because of insulin resistance, which is an acquired insensitivity to insulin signaling. However, there has also been an important trend in research to look for genes that make some humans more susceptible to T2D than others. So far, a genetic approach has failed to significantly discriminate and predict which humans would develop a complex genetic disease such as T2D but it has been more successful in the case of Mendelian diseases. Obviously, the evolutionary, homeostasis, and genetic theories are generally not in competition over the explanation of T2D. While the former is focusing on the pathophysiology of diabetes (how it works), the latter is focused on its pathogeny (how it is brought about). If one fails, the other does not necessarily prove stronger. However, they are in competition to define the specificity and the timeframe of T2D. If conceived as the disruption of homeostasis, everything before glucose levels are chronically high is better conceived as a part of the etiology and not of the pathophysiology of the disease. If conceived as a genetic disease, the pathophysiology may remain undetectable for a much longer time and the disease may start even when the deleterious effects of genes can still be compensated naturally so that no traditional sign shows. In the end, a focus on pathogeny has the effect of redefining the pathophysiology of the disease. In this, these two theories are in competition. This competition between these two theories also exists over many diseases, such as cancer, cardiovascular diseases, and neurological diseases.

These various theories also differ over the pathology-specificity of the process they describe as their object. More concretely, we may not want to consider *any* disruption of homeostasis as pathological. Perhaps hyperglycemia in type 2 diabetes is adaptive. After all, many have noted how robustly hyperglycemia is actively maintained in diabetes itself, as if it were a homeostatic process (Bernard-Weil 1999). On the other hand, if a set of mutations, or an infectious agent, or a specific property of the immune system, or of the microbiota, and so on, perfectly discriminated between those who would develop T2D and those who would not ceteris paribus, the process would indeed be specific, and the pathological status of the condition would be considered largely established. This problem exists for many other diseases which are controversially considered to be diseases – late-onset, chronic conditions such as hypertension or abnormal tissues that are sometimes labeled as "precancerous." Interestingly, the geroscience theory of disease focuses on how the specific ways in which cells and tissues are altered while we age can cause these various diseases. Many in this research program have rejected the relevance of discriminating between aging and age-related diseases on the ground that aging itself can (and should) be treated – and thus considered a pathological process, if not a disease. Others have tried to discriminate between normal and pathological aging. So far, this has mostly been speculative and has not cast much light on these questions. The reason is certainly that it has failed, so far, to concretely describe, rather than verbally refer to, the pathophysiological process of aging that is supposed to cause all these late-onset diseases.

In general, there is no space here to fully develop how these theories differ and compete over which diseases. Endorsement of one or the other explains much of the theoretical controversies, and divergences in research programs, over many diseases.

3.2 Generalizing Disease Theories

Remember that diseases entities are grouped into types – infectious diseases, metabolic diseases, cardiovascular diseases, and so on – and that most disease theories are introduced as theories of types of disease, not as theories of disease in general – although researchers expand them as much as they can. A common idea is indeed that an indefinite number of types of diseases happen to exist, and there are causes for why they exist, but no reason for why them and not others.

However, it would be naïve to believe that a disease is assigned once and for all to a disease type. In fact, theories of disease-types are possibly generalizable to more diseases than currently known. For instance, the literature on stress and diseases is huge and includes mental disorders (Heim et al. 2008; McEwen et al. 2015), cancer (Reiche et al. 2004; Heikkila et al. 2013), metabolic disorders (Karatsoreos & McEwen 2011), cardiovascular diseases (Steptoe & Kivimäki 2012), autoimmune diseases (Webster et al. 2002), and neurodegenerative disorders (Viau 2002). However, many researchers are wary of it because of the lack of experimental support of the hypothesized mechanisms and the weakness of epidemiological evidence. In contrast, the field of immunology is based on well-established mechanisms and strong epidemiological evidence. In the recent years, immunology has considerably extended its scope from a territory of diseases involving immunodeficiency, autoimmunity and excessive immune response, to an undetermined number of diseases previously categorized as neurodegenerative (Heneka et al. 2014; Heppner et al. 2015), neoplasic (Schreiber et al. 2011), metabolic (Osborn & Olefsky 2012) or vascular (Hansson & Libby 2006). Major therapeutic applications substantiate the claim, which typically involve the development of immunotherapies in new fields. Likewise, many papers have investigated the causal role of the composition or biological activity of the microbiota in diseases as different as T2D (Qin et al. 2012), cancer (Schwabe & Jobin 2013), cardiovascular diseases (Koeth et al. 2013), and autoimmune and inflammatory diseases (Belkaid & Hand 2014), but also the efficiency of immunotherapies on cancer (Routy et al. 2018) and the regulation of the immune system (Honda & Littman 2016).

More specifically, a disease theory is justified in the case of a disease D inasmuch as the process it describes is (a) necessary to D and (b) specific to the pathological phenomenon in general (i.e., takes place in diseases only). Table 4 represents how necessary the process described by each disease theory is to explain each type of disease. In this table, the darker the average color of the column, the more diseases a theory may explain. The darkest shade represents the original scope of the theory while the other colors represent its expansion. The expansion of a theory may be based on articles that apply it, or on the existence of elements to hypothesize that the process is necessary to all diseases of a type, although no article does it explicitly and systematically. Take the example of infectious diseases. The so-called Koch's postulates stipulate that a disease is infectious if and only if an infectious agent is found in all patients, is not found in subjects without the disease, and is a sufficient condition to develop the disease if

Table 4 The scope of disease theories. In columns, disease theories as listed earlier.

	Genetic theory of disease	Geroscience theory of disease	Immunological theory of disease	Stress theory of disease	Homeostasis theory of disease	DOHaD theory of disease	Evolutionary theory of disease	Microbiota theory of disease	Infectious theory of disease
01 Infectious or parasitic diseases									
02 Neoplasms									
03 Disease of the blood or blood forming organs									
04 Diseases of the immune system									
05 Endocrine, nutritional or metabolic diseases									
06 Mental, behavioural or neurodevelopmental disorders									
07 Sleep-wake disorders									
08 Diseases of the nervous system									
09 Diseases of the visual system									

Table 4 (cont.)

	Genetic theory of disease	Geroscience theory of disease	Immunological theory of disease	Stress theory of disease	Homeostasis theory of disease	DOHaD theory of disease	Evolutionary theory of disease	Microbiota theory of disease	Infectious theory of disease
10 Diseases of the ear or mastoid process									
11 Diseases of the circulatory system									
12 Diseases of the respiratory system									
13 Diseases of the digestive system									
14 Diseases of the skin									
15 Diseases of the musculoskeletal system or connective tissue									
16 Diseases of the genitourinary system									
17 Conditions related to sexual health									

18 Pregnancy, childbirth or the puerperium							
19 Certain conditions originating in the perinatal period							
20 Developmental anomalies							
21 Symptoms, signs or clinical findings, not elsewhere classified							
22 Injury, poisoning or certain other consequences of external causes							

There are papers that propose that in diseases of this group, this is a		The absence of papers proposing that it is necessary leads to conclude that it is		
Necessary and sufficient process	Necessary process in all diseases	possibly necessary	not a necessary process in all	not a necessary process in any

Lines represent types of disease after ICD-11. Shades represent how well the theory accounts for a type of disease according to the literature. More specifically, they represent

- the existence of at least one current paper that presents the process as 1) necessary and sufficient (darkest) or 2) necessary (dark) to account for all diseases of the type;
- the absence of such articles, with the conclusion that the process is 3) possibly necessary to account for all diseases of the type (medium), or 4) not necessary to some diseases of the type (light), or 5) not necessary to any disease of the type (white).

For instance, the infectious theory of disease amounts to the claim that infection may be necessary (yet undetected) in almost all types of disease, while the evolutionary theory of disease claims on theoretical ground that one of the processes it describes is necessary and sufficient or necessary in many more types of disease.

inoculated. There are many formulations of these postulates, but whatever the formulation, they do not allow for a disease to be formally characterized as infectious before a pathogen is identified. However, this allows for reasonable hypotheses that a pathogen may be involved in many apparently non-infectious diseases – think again of the example of the explanation of schizophrenia by *Toxoplasma gondii*. Beyond this, of course, there would be the merely heuristic hypothesis that *any disease* could be explained by a specific infectious agent. Finally, some theories have been proposed as a broad explanation of all diseases of a certain type, for example, the microbiota theory of disease has been applied to all neurological disorders (Cryan et al. 2019).

The extension of various theories of disease should be interpreted differently depending on the grade of necessity of the condition described for the group of diseases. Indeed, it is hard to assess how much of a disease, or of diseases, a theory can explain. An illustration of the problem is the geroscience theory of cancer: how many aspects of cancer initiation and development can the normal aging of tissues explain? Some think aging is a marginal risk factor for cancer that increases with time (e.g., through the phenomenon of inflammaging, that is, a common phenomenon of chronic inflammation with no specific reason) or that most of the causal contribution of aging is already considered in traditional theories of cancer (e.g., via the accumulation of random mutations in cells). Others consider that cancer should be conceptualized as the effect of the combination of several processes involved in the aging of a tissue. This problem of explaining a disease is frequently raised in terms of the nature of the interaction between the supposed explanatory factor, for instance, between microbiota and host (Tremaroli & Bäckhed 2012), or under the question of whether there is causation or simply association between dysbiosis and disease (de Vos & de Vos 2012). It is obviously more difficult to assess the generalizability of very recent research programs. The DOHaD agenda was named after a general explanation for metabolic disorders like T2D (Bateson et al. 2004), and it was initially applied to cardiovascular diseases (Barker 1986) before it was hypothesized to be important also for immunological and neurological disorders (Fleming et al. 2018), as well as cancer (Ekbom et al. 1992). However, the evidence is still scant. Similarly, the scope of age-related diseases is arguably limited: infectious diseases, cancer in infants, congenital disorders, and most mental disorders cannot be described as effects of aging, although aging aggravates the effects of many diseases that are not strictly speaking age-related diseases.

Importantly, disease theories do not have mutually exclusive extensions in principle – quite the contrary. In the previous subsection, I explained that the homeostasis and the genetic theories of T2D focused on different processes, and that this led to competition about where the specificity of the pathophysiology really lies. Another reason for their coexistence is that each disease theory focuses on one necessary condition – and can rarely establish that it is sufficient. If your theory is that T2D is caused by chronic nutritional imbalance, you would have to explain why some people exposed to the same or similar cause escape the effect. The same goes if your theory is that it is genetic. For that reason, there can be as many theories of processes involved as necessary conditions of a type of disease.

Most of the hype of a "new" disease theory comes from the uncertain extension of its domain of application. Just like the enthusiasm about the genetic theory of disease peaked with the achievement of the human genome project (the integral sequencing of the human genome), and the subsequent flurry of "genome-wide association studies" (systematic search for all genetic differences between populations with a disease and populations without), there has been a lot of enthusiasm around the microbiota theory of diseases, revolving around how many diseases, and how much of these diseases, it would ultimately explain.

The general point of this subsection is to warn you against the opposite, equally hasty conclusions, that the latest theory in town will necessarily explain more diseases than the previous ones or that it is bound to fail to explain all diseases. The truth is that there is no way to predict how far a theory goes. The field of physiology develops by expansion, speculation, waning, and fixation of successive research programs around specific disease theories, each of which could (in principle) be a theory of a disease type as well as a theory of disease.

3.3 Issues with the Generalization of Disease Theories

Before we get to the examination of this goal of a truly general theory of disease in the next section, it is useful to examine some issues with the potential generalization of theories of disease types.

Let us begin with a general observation. A theory of disease types usually does not come in the exact same version (T_A, T_B ...) when applied to different diseases (D_1, D_2, ... D_n). Take the example of homeostasis, a venerable and arguably general account of many diseases. Possibly all diseases can be explained as instances of disruption of homeostasis on some level, from diabetes to Down syndrome. However, applied articles with a limited scope (one form of homeostasis or one family of diseases) are much more cited than theoretical articles with a broad scope (on homeostasis in general) – including Cannon's original paper (Cannon 1929). Indeed, there is no visible overarching theoretical literature on homeostasis, as if everyone knew what it is, or conversely, considered it useless to the explanation of specific diseases. On the contrary, theories of homeostasis as one specific phenomenon are partial generalizations (e.g., Kotas & Medzhitov 2015), visible at most in one field. Another example is genetic theories of disease types. The genetic theory of hereditary and congenital iron deficiency (T_A of D_1 and D_2) is not the same as the genetic theory of infectious diseases (T_B of D_3). While the former defines a genetic disease as a process that will invariably take place, will probably take the same form since birth, and for everyone with the corresponding mutation, the latter defines a genetic disease as a susceptibility to some infectious diseases that will depend upon the encounter with the pathogen and may vary considerably depending on the strain of the pathogen and the host's age, compensatory mechanisms, and other factors. Is that really the same theory? How should it be phrased? What these two theories that apply to different diseases have in common may be much less than a unified or common theory – perhaps, simply, a vague appeal to the same ultimate explanatory terms, in this case, "gene." It is important that a common theory can be explicitly phrased. It is unavoidable that it is constantly rephrased to account, as accurately as possible, for as many phenomena as possible. For instance, a description of the process of an infectious disease, based on a currently widely accepted understanding, could be "the colonization by a pathogen of a host that generally mounts up a response in the form of a defense, involving a nonnull degree of virulence." This description may, or may not be true of cancer, depending on whether infection by pathogen X, Y, Z, cause cancer in all cases (Becsei-Kilborn 2010). But it may, or may not be true of cancer depending on how the process of infectious disease is itself described (Liu et al. 2016). For instance, it is currently not considered that any disease where a microbe intervenes is fruitfully described as an infectious disease. For instance, oncovirus-induced cancer is generally not described as such, which suggests that it may be better to describe an infectious disease as the process of colonization rather than as the simple triggering of the disease by an infection. Is this the best choice, or should the theory be rephrased in order to gain extension? No one can say before it has been tried.

More generally, the phrasing of a global disease theory faces three major conceptual difficulties that are well known to philosophers.

An **extension problem** consists in determining whether a technical term used in the description of a theory clearly applies to specific facts. For instance, "homeostasis," "allostasis," "allostatic overload," and "disruption of homeostasis" are ambiguous in many cases – is insulin resistance a case of "disruption of homeostasis" or a case of "pathological homeostasis" (Bernard-Weil 1999)? There is a theoretical discussion about whether "allostasis" really refers to something else than "homeostasis" (Day 2005). A major concept both in the evolutionary theory of disease and in the geroscience theory of disease is "antagonistic pleiotropy" (Williams 1957): namely, the hypothesis that a genetic trait has been selected for a (even modest) beneficial effect on reproduction early in life, in spite of a (even catastrophic) deleterious effect later in life. Classic but disputed examples are Huntington's disease (Shokeir 1975) and inflammation related to cancer (Campisi 2013; see the philosophical argument in Giaimo & d'Adda di Fagagna 2012). In general, it proves very difficult to determine whether a given gene is an example of antagonistic pleiotropy. "Stress" is also a notoriously difficult term to use unambiguously. What a "pathogen" is is a matter for discussion (e.g., Virgin et al. 2009). So is "mismatch" in evolutionary medicine (crucial clarification in Bourrat & Griffiths 2021). Some fields of science, like immunology, have already contributed theories meant to encompass a wide array of immune phenomena and processes as applied to many different diseases, but the exact scope of some concepts – for example, "disease tolerance" (Medzhitov et al. 2012) – remains to be investigated.

A **focal adjustment problem** consists in the choice, for a term, between a very accurate meaning with a restricted scope and a very broad scope with a vague meaning. The stress theory is highly disputed for its conceptual vagueness, which is in turn related to its potentially very broad scope. Although stress has since come to be understood as any deleterious factor acting at any level, from proteins to organisms, a properly speaking "stress theory of health and disease" is restricted to the influence of psychoneuroendocrine stress on the pathogenesis of multiple diseases. In its recent, more specific version of the allostasis theory of health and disease (McEwen 2007), it is maybe more precise but also restricted to the explanation of fewer diseases. Note that it is sometimes hard to define the conceptual framework itself in fields that tend to expand before they get precise, as is the case for DOHaD (Gluckman & Hanson 2006b). In the end, the choice of a meaning is a matter of stipulation. It should be strategic and fruitful and is always tentative. For instance, many diseases have been described as "genetic": cancer (Vogelstein & Kinzler 2004), but also bipolar disorder, coronary artery disease, Crohn's disease, rheumatoid arthritis, T1D and T2D (Wellcome Trust Case Control Consortium 2007), and many others. Philosophers have investigated both the notion of causal selection in the case of genetic diseases (Hesslow 1984; Magnus 2004) and the concept of genetic disease (Smith 2001; Darrason 2013), with particular attention to the question of the reduction to genetic explanations. They have shown that many so-called "genetic diseases" are not genetic in a strong sense, but in a weak sense in which every disease is genetic (e.g., cancer, see de Magalhães 2022). While the strong sense is both restricted to a small number of diseases and generally uncontroversial, most, if not all, diseases are likely to be of a type between pure Mendelian and "complex" in the vaguest way (Lemoine 2016). However, Darrason has proposed an original contribution by discussing not genocentrism, but the genetic theory of disease. Taking the example of the genetic theory of infectious diseases, she shows that infectious diseases are genetic as well, but not in a trivial sense.

A **consistency problem** consists in defining the key terms of a disease theory together in a coherent, but not circular way. The definitions of "pathogen," "infection," and "virulence," should be consistent with one another, but each should refer to a proper set of facts so that bringing them together does not simply follow from analysis but leads to a set of explanations and predictions. Indeed, there is a developed and precise theoretical literature in evolutionary biology, in epidemiology and in immunology that defines the basic concepts of infection. They include "pathogen" (Méthot & Alizon 2014), "host" and "parasite," "response," "defense" (Akira et al. 2006), "resistance," and "virulence" (Frank 1996). Scientists, as well as philosophers, have pointed out problems in the consistency of the microbiota theory of disease: the definition of dysbiosis, the problem of causation, and the focus on taxonomic rather than functional decomposition of the metagenome (Hooks & O'Malley 2017; Lynch et al. 2019; Greslehner 2020). The field of geroscience is not yet investigated by philosophers of science, although theoretical questions have already been listed (Lemoine 2020). A handful of philosophers have likewise discussed and contributed to the conceptual elaboration of the evolutionary theory of disease (Méthot 2011; Cournoyea 2013; Griffiths & Matthewson 2016). The microbiota theory of diseases, if it exists, still needs clarification of its main terms and their relations (Sholl et al. 2021).

Before we get to the next sections, it is useful to take stock by comparing, once again, the point of view of philosophy of physiology on the question, "what is disease?" with the point of view of traditional philosophy of medicine. The latter embraces foundationalism – the idea that the term "disease" should be defined once and for all for the field of medicine independently from its empirical discoveries – and discards disease theories. The former embraces the examination of disease theories – as potentially developing into theories of disease – and discards foundationalism. This is enough for philosophy of physiology to exist as a field, without needing to ever address such a general question as: "what is disease?" However, we also want to know what such an approach would have to say on this. Predictably, it is a much harder question to answer if you renounce foundationalism, but we are now sufficiently prepared to tackle it in the next section.

4 Toward a Theory of the Pathological Phenomenon

An intriguing fact about the pathological phenomenon is that while perhaps no specific disease will strike all individuals in a population, certainly no individual in a population will escape all diseases. Developing some diseases at some points in life seems to be a trait of all living organisms. Here are a few facts to illustrate the importance of this paradox. First, congenital diseases necessarily develop in some individuals, obviously not all of them. More generally, are some individuals bound to develop, say, cardiovascular diseases or cancer, while others are immune to these (but not others), and what roles do genes and environments play in this? Second, some diseases that happen frequently in some species, like sarcoids, a form of tumor of the skin found in horses, may be impossible in other species as far as we know. What are the physiological facts that explain these differences in the susceptibility to some disease? Third, some speculate that all human organisms – maybe mammals, animals, or even all multicellular organisms – frequently initiate cancer but efficiently inhibit its development or eradicate it most of the time. However, most admit that there is some randomness involved, so that of two individuals with the exact same genes living in the exact same environment, one may develop cancer while the other does not. How much of the pathological phenomenon depends on random events in general, how much on necessitating causes? Fourth and finally, even if it is extremely unlikely that you never catch a cold in your whole life, it is not inconceivable that you may, like it is that a human may breathe under water or survive without ever eating. If we eliminate the possibility of extreme luck, what are the differences between the hypothesis that something is missing in your physiology to develop a given disease, and the hypothesis that you have some protective mechanism actively inhibiting some part of the pathophysiological process?

I summarize these questions as follows: what makes succumbing to disease a necessary trait? A necessary trait is a trait whose presence can be derived from theoretical premises. For instance, if a sufficient cause of cancer is a certain combination of mutations (premise #1), and if there is no restriction of possible mutations (premise #2), then given infinite time, any organism will *necessarily* develop cancer eventually. We are interested in a set of theoretical claims that would explain why it is necessary that organisms have diseases in general – more specifically, why organisms are susceptible to disease. Understanding the necessity of disease that befalls living organisms is a better first step toward *one* theory of the pathological phenomenon, than is finding some universal feature – typically, ultimate consequences like suffering, dysfunction, or incapacity.

4.1 Why One Theory for All Diseases Sounds Unlikely and What It Could Achieve

Most scientists would be wary of the idea of *one* theory for *all* diseases. There are solid reasons for such skepticism. Think again of the huge variety of diseases. It is unlikely that biological properties that are common to all diseases are ever found, including those apparently so different from one another as schizophrenia and cancer. Moreover, the history of medicine strongly warns against theories of disease supposed to describe the cause of all diseases. The Hippocratic theory of dyscrasis explained all diseases by an ill-balanced mix of "humors," that is, imaginary components of the blood. The lesion theory of disease sought to explain all diseases by lesions – but some diseases appear not to be caused by any observed lesion. The same problem occurred for the germ theory of disease ("all diseases are infectious"), the psychosomatic theory of disease ("all diseases have a psychological cause"), or the genetic theory of disease ("all diseases are caused by genetic mutations"). Finally, contemporary medical research is massively specialized for a reason: the heterogeneity, complexity, and specificity of pathophysiological processes. In cancer research, for instance, one must specialize in the study of a form of cancer or even in a precise, limited process involved in a form of cancer. Even if it is still possible that encompassing theories unify pathophysiology again, specialization makes such unity both unlikely to happen and idle to seek for. So, maybe philosophers of medicine are wise to omit the possibility that a common property defines the pathophysiological, and focus instead on broad concepts like "dysfunction," or even "harm." Maybe "dysfunction" is as indifferent to the nature of many diseases as "money" is to its realization under the forms of coins, strips, cows, sheet of paper, and so on (Fodor 1974). Maybe "harm" is the same form of encompassing concept for well-established categories of diseases as the concept of "weed" is for diverse forms of plants that have nothing to do with one another biologically (Cooper 2005).

However, we have seen in Section 2 that the huge variety of specific diseases results from the many combinations of relatively few unspecific pathophysiological processes. We also emphasized that these processes are causally connected. We entertained the view of the pathological phenomenon as one "bush" of connected processes, and concluded that in this case, the unity of pathophysiology is not to be sought in analogous features of infinitely varied diseases, but in their underlying, causal processes. We also insisted that it is natural and useful to try to extend to other diseases a theory that explains some diseases well. The proposal, in the present section, is not to focus on a unitary pathophysiology of all diseases, but on the common causes to all pathophysiological processes – a theory of these causes would be a theory of disease.

4.2 The Conceptual Necessity of the Pathological Phenomenon

Before we investigate general causes of the pathological phenomenon, we must examine one important consequence of the variability of traits for the necessity of disease.

Organisms of the same species are similar but not identical – some have bigger bodies, move their wings faster, reproduce more quickly, are more vulnerable to cold, operate photosynthesis more efficiently, and so on than others. These are variations in traits. Any population of living organisms presenting variations in traits can be represented as a distribution of the probability that the bearer survives, or reproduces, or that the traits are more frequent in the next generation. Physiology is not primarily interested in whether a trait tends to be more frequent in a population with time – this is a crucial question for evolutionary biology. Physiologists are primarily interested in whether variations affect individual survival (and possibly, reproduction). An important consequence is that there will necessarily be a lower tail of contributive traits – that is, some variations will perform poorly as compared to others. Diseases fall in the category of variations that perform comparatively poorly.

This fact has been taken as a defining feature of disease, creating unsolvable problems. Should we, or should we not, call all extreme variations that are deleterious to survival "diseases," or should we introduce a threshold and/or standard environmental conditions? If we accept the premise, then disease is conceptually necessary for trivial reasons. For instance, if we imagine that all the diseases we know were made impossible in some mutant organism, a new population of such mutant organisms that present variations in performance affecting survival would be sufficient to reintroduce disease susceptibility. Reciprocally, in that view, it is conceptually impossible that a specific, congenital disease is universal – indeed, there is always an upper end to the distribution of any functional trait, except when a radical change in the environment universally reduces the probability of survival to zero.

Our perspective should be different. Variability in traits contribution to survival is *one* of the theoretical premises from which the necessity of disease derives. However, it would be completely trivial if we took the lower-end tail to be the *defining* feature of disease. In any possible world where there is variability in trait contribution, there would be diseases. We are interested instead in the natural world where other, more specific and less trivial conditions make susceptibility to disease a necessary fact and explain the variations of that susceptibility across species and populations. We should therefore extend our investigation beyond this premise and its necessary consequence.

4.3 The Fourfold Root of the Natural Necessity of the Pathological Phenomenon

The investigation of general, common causes of the existence of the pathological phenomenon has been initiated by evolutionary medicine. Evolutionary medicine is a research program defined as "a growing and central discipline that applies evolutionary knowledge to the understanding of human biology, both normal and abnormal. It is an essential science, necessary for a holistic perception of how health and disease emerge." (Gluckman et al. 2009). Here, we will focus on the natural causes that make disease necessary in any, or most, species. If the pathological phenomenon in any species can be represented as a bush, we may compare its general causes to the roots. Many contributors have listed these general causes differently. As an introductory hypothesis to illustrate this approach to a theory of disease, I propose to reinterpret the original quadripartition proposed by Williams and Nesse (1991) in their seminal paper. The four roots of the pathological phenomenon, that is, the causes that make us necessarily vulnerable to diseases, I will propose, can be described under the labels of "mismatch," "infection," "disposability" and "senescence."

Mismatch is a crucial concept for evolutionary medicine. Because species evolve and environments change, mismatches between organisms (or genes) and environments are unavoidable. Most famously, contemporary humans present maladapted traits selected in the environment of the Pleistocene (i.e., the Environment of Evolutionary Adaptedness, or EEA, which ended some 12,000 years ago). Yet their environment has massively changed: climatic stability, changes in nutritional patterns due to the emergence of agriculture, food abundance, sedentary life, social demands, and so on have generated several cases of mismatch responsible for frequent diseases – typically, metabolic diseases, hypertension, cancers, and so on. Importantly, diseases are necessary because mismatches are unavoidable. There is no way organisms can be equally fit in *all* possible environments. Adaptation through evolution by natural selection will take time. Philosophers have clarified this concept of mismatch and insisted on how sound a theoretical basis it provides to the development of evolutionary medicine (Bourrat & Griffiths 2021). Importantly, note that the conceptual necessity of a distribution of differential fitness superimposes on the unavoidability of mismatch. Indeed, even widespread "maladapted" traits such as tooth decay due to excess sugar intake, blood pressure due to salty diet, and so on are unevenly distributed in a population. Maladaptedness is therefore a doubly relative concept: as compared to the average EEA human, and within current human populations. However, note that a radical mismatch can strike a whole population relatively evenly through extreme environmental change. Mismatch is the first root of the pathological phenomenon and the first principle to account for its necessity.

Infection is the second root of the pathological phenomenon and the second cause that makes disease necessary. Williams and Nesse have insisted on the concept of "arms race" between host and pathogen, but they have not really addressed the question of the necessity that there are infectious diseases. A hypothesis is that infection is made possible by common ancestry of all living organisms. Consequently, species can hardly be so heterogeneous as to not interact chemically with one another. They use the same resources and build similar molecules thanks to largely identical processes – for instance, viruses share RNA or DNA molecules with mammals and plants. For that reason, molecules built by some species can be used by others, and processes performed in some can be hijacked by others to the former's profit, with the outcome of disease for the latter. In fact, this form of disease is not necessary in a strong sense, as shown by the possibilities of mutualism or symbiosis. Yet, as there is reciprocally no necessity of mutualism or symbiosis and a very high number of occurrences of such chemical competition, an infectious disease is so likely to occur at some point that it can be considered a necessity in practice. Moreover, as there are populational variations in responses to infection and in virulence, the lower-tail view of disease also applies to infectious diseases – some will be affected, others not enough to be considered sick. Note also that not every individual is necessarily infected at a given time, but that all can be and thus a disease can be universal. Although infection can be conceptualized as a specific form of mismatch, it is a root of its own regarding the necessity of disease.

The third root of the pathological phenomenon can be called *disposability*. Indeed, organisms have to face physical and chemical forces of destruction in general – the evolutionary cause of disease Williams and Nesse call "injuries and intoxications." There is no way they could evolve perfect defenses against all injuries. Not only is this unlikely to be physically feasible, but natural selection would favor any improvement in individual reproductive value over any improvement of longevity, in the face of any trade-off between these two traits. This is the idea of the so-called "disposable soma theory" (Kirkwood & Holliday 1979).[7] In a nutshell, an optimal balance is selected, in the variations of a species, between investing resources in immediate reproduction and investing resources in individual maintenance and repair that increases lifespan and chances of future reproduction. The necessity of reproduction and the challenges it faces together explain that a species must limit repair and maintenance to the strict minimum

---

[7] More specifically, the disposable soma theory claims that senescence is explained by disposability. For that reason, it was introduced as a theory of aging. Here, I simply follow Williams and Nesse, and propose that the disposable soma theory is better understood as the expression of this third root of the pathological phenomenon than as an explanation of the necessity of aging.

required to ensure reproduction, depending on their vulnerability to their environment. This necessary fallibility of repair and maintenance partially overlaps with two forms of mismatch, "developmental" and "physiological mismatch" (Bourrat & Griffiths 2021). Just like infection, the disposability of individual organisms can be interpreted as a form of mismatch. However, just like infection, it is a distinct root of the necessity of disease. Moreover, the conceptual necessity of a distribution in a population also applies to disposability. That is, individuals may have different abilities to maintain or repair, or to invest in repair or maintenance at any stage of their life, or in the face of a specific challenge. In the end, variable disposability also explains in part how organisms respond to, and survive, infectious diseases. Indeed, either infection or a response to infection generally involves tissue destruction.

The fourth root of the necessity of disease is *senescence*. It is also the only one not to be universal. Indeed, not all species are senescent. There can be no age-related diseases in non-senescent species (by definition). Reciprocally, there must be age-related degradations, dysfunctions, or diseases, in senescent species. Senescence may have emerged from a form of antagonistic pleiotropy – as a trait with early beneficial effects on development and reproduction and late deleterious effects on survival (Williams 1957). "Early" and "late" are defined relative to the reproductive period of life. A senescent trait is indeed unlikely to ever produce its late deleterious effect, while its early, favorable effect is readily selected. During evolution, senescence thus appeared as the side effect of multiple ways to lower the risk of early death, including of early disease, whatever its form. Senescence is also yet another form of mismatch, but a specific cause of the necessity of diseases – the diseases that are commonly called "age-related" (in relevant species). Moreover, it interacts with both infectability and disposability. Lastly, the lower-tail conception of disease also applies here. First, variations in a population of all ages also produce a distribution, which is likely to correspond to the distribution of individuals of that population according to age. More specifically, the lower tail of the distribution is likely to coincide with the old. In a longitudinal perspective, all individuals are less functional than they used to be when they enter old age. Second, in a subpopulation of the old, there is, again, a distribution – the lower tail of which can be interpreted as that of the diseased. For these two reasons, the conceptual necessity of disease introduced in the previous subsection is the source of a classical controversy over whether aging is a disease. Individuals decline over time and the lower tail of distributions of traits corresponds to the old or to the worse off of the old, which leads to interpreting the processes that explain their conditions as diseases.

Figure 4 graphically represents the action of the four roots of the pathological phenomenon, along with the lower-tail aspect of disease, as they are traditionally

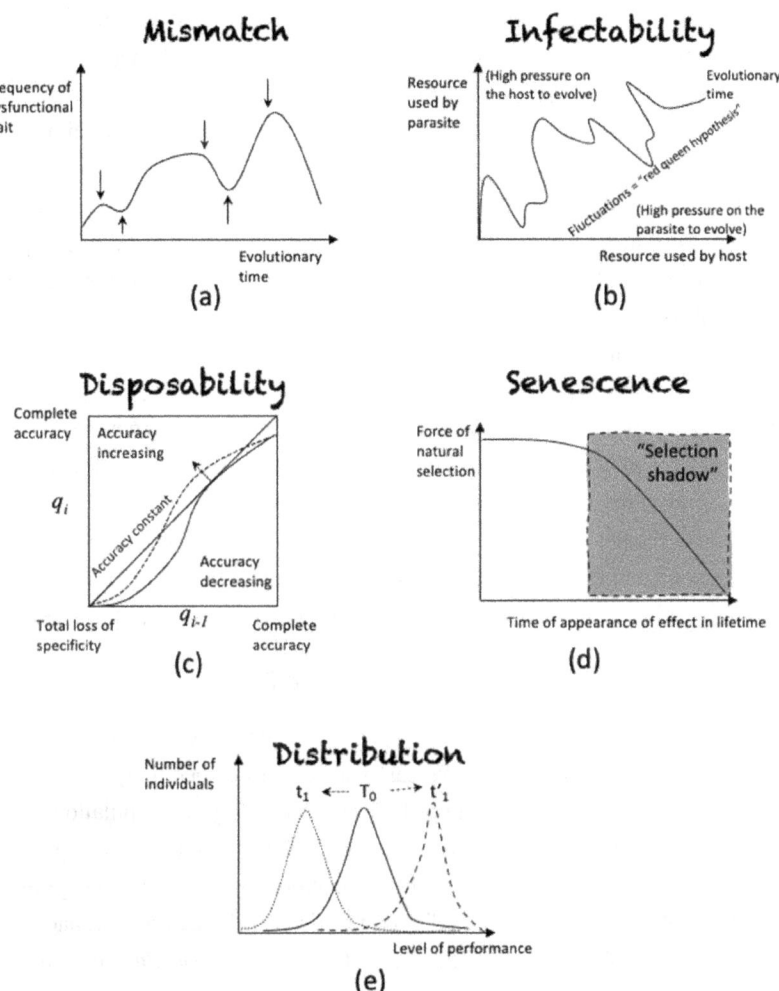

Figure 4 Represents how the various evolutionary answers to the question: "why are there diseases?" (a) Changes in genes or environment (arrows) affect the level of dysfunctional traits. When more frequent, *mismatch* ensues. (b) Hosts and parasites necessarily compete for resources, which leads to host *infectability*. With changes of the balance, selective pressure increases alternatively on one or the other, representing the "arms race" of the "red queen hypothesis." (c) *Disposability* is the fact that replicated proteins at generation q_i are not identical to proteins at generation q_{i-1} resulting in a loss of accuracy. This is necessary because an increase in accuracy is useless for reproduction (after Kirkwood 1977). (d) *Senescent* traits, that is, with late onset deleterious effects, cannot be eliminated due to the decrease of selective pressure at the time in life when they appear – the "selection shadow." (e) With time and circumstances, distribution of levels of performance may change (from t_0 to either t_1 or t'_1), but there always is a Gaussian *distribution*.

represented in the scientific literature. However, there is still some way to go toward a theory of the pathological phenomenon. I have sketched how these roots may intermingle into the production of some of the properties of the pathological phenomenon. This is enough to substantiate the idea of a theory explaining why diseases are necessary.

The next question is that of a unified theory of disease. Figure 5 represents three possibilities. The "one trunk" theory of disease (Figure 5, top) suggests that all the roots of the pathological phenomenon combine into one process from which all types of diseases branch out. This strong claim would undoubtedly establish the unity of the phenomenon and justify the idea that there is one theory of disease. The "few offshoots" theory of disease (Figure 5, middle) is that a limited number of combinations of the four roots explain why the diseases that we know exist. It is still compatible with the claim that there is one theory of disease, provided that the combinations are not too many. Finally, the "many offshoots" theory of disease (Figure 5, bottom) is the least favorable to the existence of one theory of disease. According to this theory, the causes of the necessity of disease do not account for their variety in any significant way.

4.4 The Idea of Disease Profiles

Why there is disease at all, is not the only question we can profitably ask a theory of disease to answer. We can also ask more specific questions, such as why certain diseases are more or less frequent in a given population.

Indeed, populations, human or otherwise, have specific "disease profiles," that is, a pattern of diseases with their prevalence, incidence, average age of onset, lethality, and so on. Such a disease profile also characterizes a space of the possible states of disease, and likely trajectories in this space, for individuals in the population. Obviously, the distribution of the various diseases is not random, that is, they are not equally frequent. Some underlying causes must produce patterns with a certain degree of necessity, notwithstanding a certain variety of disease profiles.

Let's take a specific example. Aging is a major determinant of the distribution of diseases in senescent species (as is obvious in Figure 6b in the case of humans). Physiological reasons would explain why the same age-related diseases may not strike all species in the same proportions in protected environments. While infectious diseases kill more individuals in aged populations than in the young, the proportion of death by infections remains surprisingly constant after the first year of life (see Figure 6a). These are some of the causes of the disease profile of a population. A disease profile has also specific, necessary consequences. In human populations, what is called the "burden of disease"

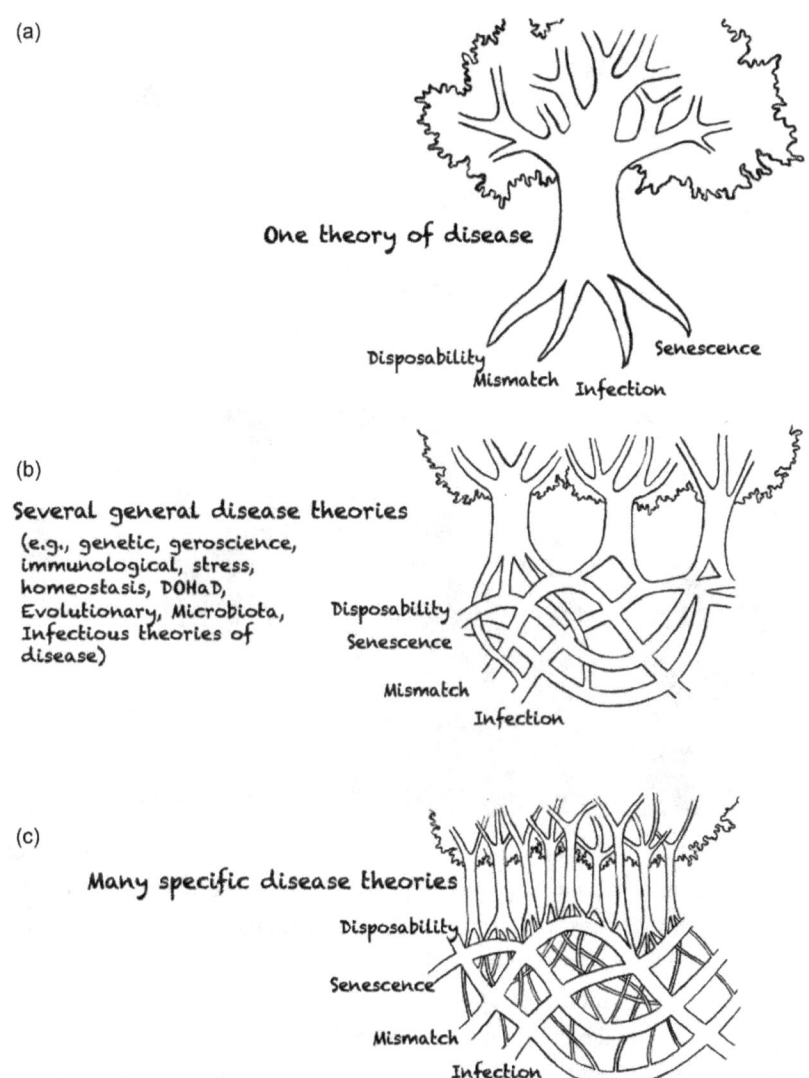

Figure 5 Three versions of the roots of disease, (a) with a universalized disease theory ("one trunk theory"), (b) with several disease theories ("few offshoots theory"), and (c) with no general disease theory but many specific disease theories ("many offshoots theory").

measures some of them. Whereas the risk of a disease for a given age is a probability measured by incidence, the burden of disease for a given age takes incidence, prevalence, fatality, impairment, and social and economic costs into account. It can be estimated for a specific disease – say cancer (Thun et al. 2018) – or all diseases. Finally, a disease profile is also characterized by

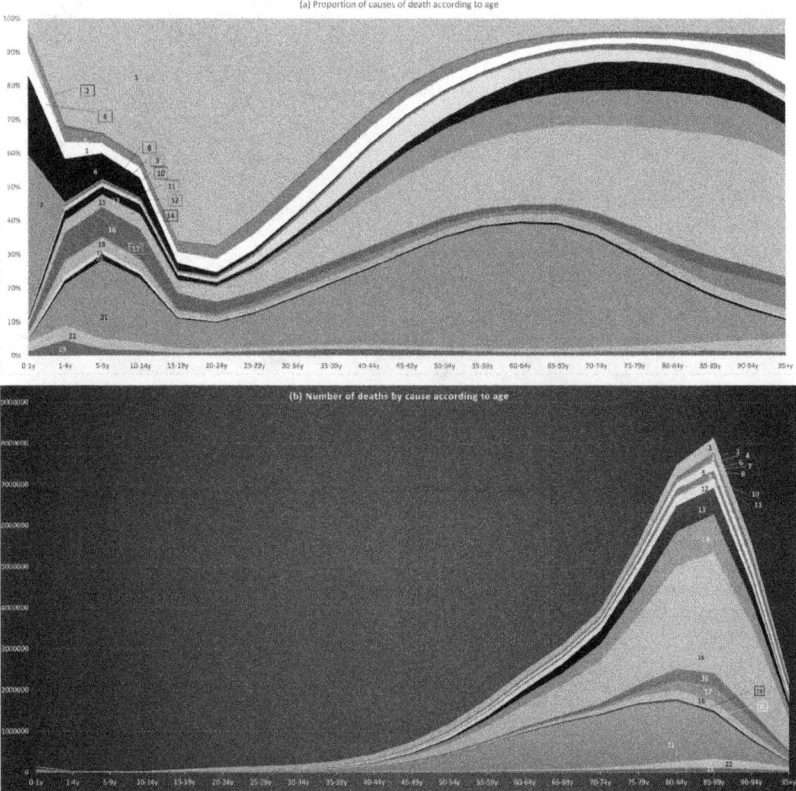

Figure 6 Death by disease in the E.U. between 2011 and 2017. (a) Proportion of causes of death according to age, (b) frequency of causes of death according to age 01 All extrinsic causes of death; 02 Other symptoms, signs and abnormal clinical and laboratory findings (remainder of R00-R99; 03 Ill-defined and unknown causes of mortality; 04 Sudden infant death syndrome; 05 Symptoms, signs and abnormal clinical and laboratory findings, not elsewhere classified (R00-R99); 06 Congenital malformations, deformations and chromosomal abnormalities (Q00-Q99); 07 Certain conditions originating in the perinatal period (P00-P96); 08 Pregnancy, childbirth and the puerperium (O00-O99); 09 Diseases of the genitourinary system (N00-N99); 10 Diseases of the musculoskeletal system and connective tissue (M00-M99); 11 Diseases of the skin and subcutaneous tissue (L00-L99); 12 Diseases of the digestive system (K00-K93); 13 Non-infectious respiratory; 14 Ischaemic heart diseases; 15 Diseases of the circulatory system (I00-I99); 16 Diseases of the nervous system and the sense organs (G00-H95); 17 Mental and behavioural disorders (F00-F99); 18 Endocrine, nutritional and metabolic diseases (E00-E90); 19 Diseases of the blood and blood-forming organs and certain disorders involving the immune mechanism; 20 Non-malignant neoplasms

complex interactions between the various diseases that strike a population in a given time and place – what the historian of medicine Mirko Grmek called "pathocenose" (Grmek 1969).

Aging explains important properties of the disease profile of senescent species (see Figure 6b again). Biodemography is the biological investigation of the demography of human longevity as compared to longevity in other species (for a survey of the field, see Wachter 2008). It studies the patterns and causes of death in a population. Biodemography has been built around the Gompertz-Makeham model of mortality (Olshansky 2010). According to this model, mortality is explained by the combination of two factors: extrinsic and intrinsic causes of death. Extrinsic causes of death are contingent and environmental. They group factors such as predation, hunger, thirst, poisoning, or injuries. Their incidence does not depend on age, at least in adult life. Intrinsic causes of death are necessary and organismal. They comprise aging and diseases.[8] The incidence of intrinsic causes of death tends to increase exponentially with age in a senescent population. This makes disease a necessary cause of death in two different senses. In both non-senescent and senescent species, it is necessary by chance that individuals die from a disease in the long run (as a face will sooner or later obtain in an infinite series of rolls of the dice). In senescent species alone, as humans are, disease is a necessary cause of death simpliciter, that is, it determines, independently of circumstances, a maximum lifespan of the species.

A major effect of diseases in human populations is indeed death. While environmental mismatch, infectious diseases, injuries and intoxication are major killers in most species, including senescent species, age-related diseases have become the major cause of death in human populations of developed countries. In fact, the three other causes of death are extrinsic and highly controllable; aging is not – or not as easily. Moreover, remarkably few diseases kill the aged in such populations (see Figure 6a). There may be a necessity that, in a shielded environment, most humans die from neoplasm, arterial lesions, or infections of the upper respiratory tract; some inbred strains of lab mice also die particularly frequently of neoplasm (Szymanska et al. 2014).

Caption for Figure 6 (cont.)

(benign and uncertain); 21 Neoplasms; 22 Infectious respiratory; 23 Certain infectious and parasitic diseases (A00-B99)

(**Source:** Eurostat. Design by Peppina Zimmermann).

---

[8] Biodemography considers infection as an intrinsic cause of death, but the cause of infection as environmental. On the other hand, it does not consider poisoning or injuries as the trigger of an intrinsic cause of death.

4.5 A Shorthand Recapitulation on Disease

It may be useful to summarize the synoptic view of disease we have sketched in this section and put it into some perspective.

(1) Disease is a necessary, not contingent, cause of limitation of the longevity of all living beings. It results from natural selection. In non-senescent species, this limitation is extrinsic but will necessarily happen in the long run under one form or another, for example, due to environmental mismatch, infection, or imperfect repair. In senescent species, an additional, intrinsic cause of limitation to longevity is aging. It makes disease physiologically necessary in these species. These four roots of disease are independent, but as factors, they combine and, generally, potentialize one another. In principle, all diseases should stem from (at least one of) these four roots (see Figure 5).

(2) The question of one theory of disease is whether these four roots join into a single trunk before they branch into specific diseases, combine into a limited number of trunks, thus giving few types of diseases, or produce an indefinite number of trunks, mostly indifferently to how the necessity of disease is accounted for.

(3) The high diversity of diseases in a population should not hide the regularity necessitated by deep causes common to all diseases. Aging is one obvious cause of such regularity. It explains that the incidence of diseases, and the incidence of lethal diseases, increases exponentially with time. It combines with disposability to produce "age-related diseases." It also casts light on the difference between easily controllable diseases – mainly, due to extrinsic causes – and uncontrollable diseases – due to intrinsic causes. This difference explains the so-called epidemiological transition (from acute to chronic disease as the main cause of death in human populations).

(4) Disease is also the conceptually necessary result of the existence of variability in functional traits. Variability is an important and almost universal factor of disease. Some propose that the least functional variations are always defined as diseases, and no matter how highly functional a species may become, it will always be composed of a lower tail of less functional individuals. Others require an additional condition to restrict this lower-tail conception to some phenomena only.

This sketch should not be taken as a hypothetical definition to be proven right or wrong by cases traditionally considered to be "diseases." Rather, it may prove a starting point for theorizing about the pathological phenomenon in all its generality and in its necessity.

5 Toward a Theory of Physiological Health

If you go to a doctor for a check up, and the doctor says you are healthy, what they generally mean is that you simply have no disease they can detect. In this sense, it seems that "health" does not really refer to some present property, process, or thing, but to the absence of many – diseases that you do not have. A common and apparently reasonable interpretation is thus to assume that if diseases are certainly an object of physiological science, health is not. "Strictly speaking, there is no science of health" (Canguilhem 1991). Many doctors would admit that they know what diabetes or cancer is, but not what health is. However, health itself surely is a natural fact as well, and not only a concept. First, health is the functioning of the body when there is no disease, or it is related to a certain subset of these functions. Second, health is what you want to improve through diet and physical activity. Moreover, you may want to improve specific aspects of your health. If you run long distance, you may want to improve your maximum oxygen consumption, which in turn should reflect your endurance, as it depends on your cardiovascular health. If you practice rugby, you may want to increase your muscle mass. In the former case, you will also want to lose weight to the level compatible with your best speed, while in the latter case, you may prioritize a gain of weight compatible with a sufficient level of speed. These are different forms that health can take. Each state we may want to reach relies on physiological interdependencies that can be investigated and make them realizable or not, with a certain number of short-term and long-term consequences we may also want to know. In investigating these interdependencies and consequences, we are investigating health itself. In all its generality, health is about how organisms breathe, digest, perceive, move, and grow. Even with a disease, health is present in an organism. This is the object of physiology. In a narrower sense, your health is only a subset of physiological capacities – namely, your capacity to maintain, preserve, restore all physiological capacities, as it is supported by specific mechanisms.

In this section, we investigate physiology – now, as the science of health. We should expect it to be very different from the concept of health central to other disciplines such as population health and public health. Philosophers have already proposed multiple explications of this population concept of health: the "welfare theory of health" (Nordenfelt 1995), the capability conception of health (Whitbeck 1981; Venkatapuram 2013), conative theories of health (Raibley 2013) or life course theory (Valles 2018). Such conceptions may be involved in important questions in public health (Kershnar 2016) and are crucial in the interpretation of various measurements in population health (Hausman 2012). In this section, we want to examine a different concept of health than *public/population* health, namely: *physiological* health (Ayres 2020). I first distinguish health as normal physiology from dedicated functions intended to restore it when it is challenged (5.1), then investigate them in turn as what I respectively call "material homeostasis" (5.2) and "mechanisms" of health (5.3). The last three subsections introduce vexed conceptual questions for scientists: the variability of health (5.4), the limits of the concept of homeostasis (5.5), and the relationship between health and the evolutionary concept of fitness (5.6).

5.1 The Two Objects of a Physiological Science of Health

What is physiological health?

A first, natural interpretation is that "health" refers to the normal functioning of organisms, which is the primary object of physiology. So far, we have focused on pathophysiology, which is a part of physiology (in the broad sense). The physiological science of normal functions is often called "physiology" (in a stricter sense), and, rarely, "normophysiology." In fact, scientists sometimes say that a process is "physiological" to emphasize that it is healthy or normal or, at least, not pathological.[9] In this general sense, "health" is how organisms survive and, maybe, reproduce. Physiology (in the strict sense) is the science of breathing and digesting, of moving and perceiving, and so on; the science of what epithelia in the lungs and stomach, the muscular tissue and the sensory and motor nerves, and so on, do; the science of what the cells that constitute these tissues, organs and systems, contribute.

Following that interpretation, many have considered that, just as in medical practice, "health" simply refers to the privation of disease. In physiology, "disease" becomes the privation of health. More specifically, you can infer that someone is probably healthy from the absence of any detectable disease, but you must determine what the normal physiology should be if you want to define a process as pathophysiological. Based on that observation, an apparently sound inference is that the two concepts are complementary and perfectly reversible. Yet this is inaccurate, as several philosophers have noted (Whitbeck 1981; Nordenfelt 1995; Lemoine 2009). Surely, it is difficult to think of one physiological function for which there is no known corresponding dysfunction, so that our knowledge of functions seems to be implied in our knowledge of dysfunctions. Moreover, it is true that, in theory, any function can fail. However, the science of health and the science of disease are to some extent independent. First, there are many non-pathological variations in "health" in this broad sense that we seek to understand – sports physiology,

---

[9] More specifically, "physiology" both refers to a method of explanation and to an object of scientific investigation, that is, the biological phenomena that can be healthy or pathological (Lemoine & Pradeu 2018).

which studies how and why some run faster or longer than others without the latter having diseases, for instance, is a good example of a part of the science of physiological health that has no pathophysiological counterpart. Second, there are many possible dysfunctions for the same normal function (e.g., there can be several causes for why a patient cannot move a finger), so that knowing normal function will not be sufficient to deduce any knowledge of dysfunctions. Even more specifically, a pathophysiological process has its own course which is not strictly determined by, and could therefore not have been predicted from, the normal physiology of the organism (Nervi 2010): for instance, cancer development has its own logic (if any "logic" at all) that is, precisely, no more contained in the normal functioning of the tissue, than you could deduce that something is shifting from red to blue from the fact that it is "not white." Finally, it makes sense, and is certainly useful, to consider that health and disease may both be found in the same organism at the same time, even if they antagonize one another: "a high degree of health is compatible with some degree of disease, injury and impairments" (Whitbeck 1981).

More recently, a different interpretation of "health" has emerged in physiological science (Ayres 2020; López-Otín & Kroemer 2021). As opposed to the whole functioning of organisms, "health" may refer to a specific subset of adaptive capacities – intuitively, the capacities to recover, repair, regenerate, and self-maintain. During most of their life, humans have imperfect repair mechanisms (e.g., leaving scars in wounded tissues) and no regeneration mechanisms (they do not grow limbs back). Having no *bauplan*, sponges can alternatively regenerate a damaged area or grow in some other direction. Planarians can and will regenerate entirely from a small subset of cells. This is one way these different metazoans actively maintain their health. Why do humans maintain theirs differently? For instance, why can skin cells of placental animals efficiently repair some DNA damage but not UVA damage to pyrimidine while other animals, plants and fungi use photolyase to that end (Miles et al. 2020)? These are questions about health in this stricter sense. In this sense, health is an even more independent object from disease than in the broader sense: it is a specific subset of mechanisms, whose function is precisely to deal with diseases and injuries. "The evolved mechanisms of health are distinct from disease pathogenesis mechanisms," notes Ayres, so that we should "develop an understanding of the biology of physiological health" (Ayres 2020). In this sense again, there can even be "diseases of health," that is, dysfunctions of the mechanisms of health (e.g., the inability to repair UV damage or to form a scar).

5.2 Homeostasis

"Homeostasis" is the technical translation of the vernacular concept of health, both in the broad and in the narrow sense, as defined earlier – a physiological reconstruction of "health."[10] A simple example of homeostasis is the regulation of body temperature. Some animals, called "homeotherms," have mechanisms to actively regulate their body temperature so that it is maintained within a certain range, increased when it is cold outside (e.g., by shivering), decreased when it is hot (e.g., by sweating): this balance is called "homeostatic." This captures the broad sense of "health" because all functions are maintained by some sort of homeostasis, and the narrow sense because all the mechanisms of health just defined actively produce a form of homeostasis.

"Homeostasis" is also understood in two senses: *formal* and *material*. In the *formal* sense developed in cybernetics (Wiener 1948; Bertalanffy 1969), the term refers to any type of process where a feedback loop actively intervenes to restore a given variable to a given range of values (a thermostat, climate, and many more systems, living or not, are homeostatic in that sense). In the *material* sense, "homeostasis" refers to one specific, optimized balance an organism can supposedly remain in indefinitely, which includes defined processes and a precise range of quantitative values. The science of material homeostasis is the science of the specific ways organisms have evolved homeostasis, related to precise variables, and certain effects – from how cells maintain the level of proteins they need ("proteostasis") or their pH, to how ecosystems regulate populations.

In the formal sense, it is easy to define and detect homeostasis. In fact, it is so easy that characterizing a system as "homeostatic" does not say much. Surely, health is homeostatic, but so are many pathological conditions as well, such as metabolic syndrome, cancer, but also hypertension and hypothyroidism. These pathological states keep their own balance. In the last two examples, the range of base values and the boundaries that serve as reference – of blood pressure and thyroid hormones respectively – is simply shifted to the right.

In the material sense, homeostasis in an organism is one complex, multidimensional balance that encompasses a range of coordinated states of the various components of the organism at any level. By definition, these states exclude pathological states that are homeostatic in the formal sense, like metabolic syndrome, hypertension, hypothyroidism, and cancer, because they will disrupt material homeostasis sooner or later (or at some level). In the material sense,

---

[10] Boorse has left the meaning and role of homeostasis unclear in his account of health and disease, first rejecting it somewhat surprisingly (Boorse 1977), then acknowledging its importance and claiming that it was implicit in his account (Boorse 1997). An explication of Boorse's biostatistical theory of health and disease in terms of homeostasis has been proposed (Dussault & Gagné-Julien 2015).

homeostasis is difficult to define and detect (and may not even exist). A complete description would require that the whole of physiology is integrated.[11] In fact, hypothesizing that a number of processes and values are a part of homeostasis in that sense is crucial to medicine. Think of the use made of "homeostasis" in intensive care, which involves a limited list of vital signs (O_2 saturation, heart rate, blood pressure, temperature, calcium level, etc.). It is a reasonable hypothesis that when values of these vital signs are controlled, the patient is "stable" and will survive. However, any doctor knows that this hypothesis is a simplification, as many more unknown determinants can defeat the prediction. One of the results of progress in medical science is to provide a still more comprehensive and predictive description of homeostasis.

It is the material sense, not the formal sense of homeostasis, that explains why humans can survive circumstance X but not circumstance Y, how long they live, why some can perform certain functions at such a level while others cannot, and why the phenomenon of disease impairs various abilities.

One major difference between the formal and the material sense of homeostasis, is that while in the formal sense, any balanced or self-regulated subsystem of an organism can be properly called homeostatic in itself, in the material sense, this subsystem may only participate in homeostasis – or not. A striking illustration is when the same variables are balanced differently in different subsystems of the same organism. Tissue homeostasis in the liver involves the same actors and processes as tissue homeostasis in the epidermis, muscle, bone marrow, or epithelium of the gut: stem cells, differentiated cells, apoptosis, proliferation, senescence, and inflammation, to mention a few. Yet in each of these systems, the balance is different, with different effects, for example, on the rate of cell renewal. While inflammation is generally not a *constant* component of homeostasis in most organs, it is constantly participating in it in the liver or the gut. While the formal sense would hardly help determine whether cell renewal is too quick or inflammation too high in a system that is homeostatic all the same, the material sense will determine how the same components should behave homeostatically in different tissues. Moreover, physiology in general, and medicine in particular, would be deprived of a major concept if it could not determine what the contribution of one system can be to homeostasis and thereby how long a regime of life can last with what consequences.

---

[11] One possible complete material description is: growth and development, macro-/micronutrient and vitamin regulation, socialization, thermoregulation, energy balance – appetite, energy balance – body composition, detoxification, osmoregulation, acid–base balance, and oxygenation (Ayres 2020).

5.3 Mechanisms of Health

The two articles mentioned earlier (5.1) converge in trying to push the science of homeostasis further by detailing what the mechanisms of health are. That said, their scope is different. López-Otín and Kroemer have the broadest view on the mechanisms of health while Ayres goes further in the direction of theorizing them.

Ayres' proposal is not a full-fledged theory of health but consists in theoretical distinctions that are preparing such a theory. She introduces the theorization with the striking results of an experiment her team carried out: when healthy, genetically identical rodents are faced with the challenge of a dose of the pathogen *C. rodentium* sufficient to kill half of them stochastically, the half that shows no sign of disease and survives has the same high pathogen burden as the half that is deteriorating and eventually dies. To fully understand this, she introduces this notion of health mechanisms as distinct from disease mechanisms. What explains the difference in survival must be a difference in the health mechanisms. More generally, she proposes to distinguish two broad types of mechanisms of health. On the one hand, *defensive health mechanisms*, that are active only against a challenge, and on the other hand, *homeostatic health mechanisms*, that are always active. In the experiment earlier, both may explain the difference, but defensive health mechanisms are more likely to explain it. These defensive mechanisms in turn either *antagonize* or *withstand* insults. They antagonize insults by *avoidance* – a behavioral mechanism to stay away from, say, a pathogen – or *resistance* – a mechanism to eradicate a pathogen once infected. Neither explains what happened in the experiment. Defensive mechanisms withstand insults by *tolerance* – compensating for the effects of the disease – or *neutralization* – for instance, detoxifying by purifying the blood from the toxin produced by a pathogen (but not the pathogen itself). Either one or the other must have happened in this experiment. These mechanisms of defensive health either produce *maintenance* – the level of health remaining the same throughout the challenge – or *resilience* – the capacity to recover health after the challenge has impaired it. In turn, homeostatic mechanisms include *homeostatic control mechanisms* – mechanisms that actively restore an intrinsic variable (e.g., heart rate or blood pressure) – and *homeostatic tolerance mechanisms* – mechanisms that compensate for the failure to maintain or restore the normal value of an intrinsic variable. Homeostatic mechanisms have the effect of *promoting vigor* (health under normal unchallenged conditions) and *apparent vigor*, that is, vigor maintained at the cost of some other detrimental change, for example, cardiac hypertrophy is the enlargement of the heart that may happen to maintain cardiac output when compensating for high blood pressure, with lethal long-term consequences. Note also that these homeostatic mechanisms participate in homeostasis but are not homeostasis itself – namely, a general mechanism of balance that is, in physiology, the naturalized version of "health," in the broader sense of normal functioning just explained.

López-Otín and Kroemer distinguish three families of "stigmata" of health: *spatial compartmentalization, maintenance of homeostasis over time*, and *adequate responses to stress*. Spatial compartmentalization contains both the *integrity of barriers* at all levels of the organism (think of the membrane of the nucleus within our cells, of the cell membrane, of an epithelium consisting in tightly jointed cells, of the blood vessels, the skin, etc.) and the *containment of perturbations*, that is, active processes that antagonize the spread of a harmful process (the formation of a cyst, the destruction of an infected cell, the formation of a scar, etc.). Maintenance of homeostasis over time consists in mechanisms of *recycling and turnover* (as most of the components of a part of the organism need to be replaced at some point), *integration of circuitry* (as systems must communicate within the organism) and *rhythmic oscillations* (many processes must keep a regular pattern – think of the alternance of wake and sleep). Finally, responses to stress contain *repair and regeneration, hormetic regulation* – hormesis is usually defined as the property of improving through exposure to limited stress – and *homeostatic resilience*. These distinctions come as an open list where Ayres' distinctions look more systematic and exhaustive. However, Ayres' distinctions are somewhat dependent on the specific context of immunology, and it is not always clear how other mechanisms would fit into her classification. In contrast, López-Otín and Kroemer give very diverse examples from different fields and at all levels of organization. Either paper illustrates how vast and rich a science of physiological health in this narrow sense can be. Their approach also emphasizes that health can be considered an evolved (complex) trait, not just a label that summarizes all the physiology of normal functions.

5.4 Does Homeostasis Capture the Variability of Health?

As you may know from your own experience, blood pressure, heart rate, and sweating must generally increase to sustain physical effort. During pregnancy as well, or sleep, or digestion, or exposure to cold weather, and so on, a whole range of variables are maintained within different boundaries than the usual values. You may think that your health is unlikely to be *one* perfect and ideally invariable balance. Certainly, these are all homeostatic in the formal sense, but the material sense of homeostasis seems to grossly contrast one ideal state with all other possible states, without accommodating for individual specificities, degrees, multiplicity, or adaptability. In this sense, homeostasis may be, at best, a pragmatic simplification for clinical use – useless or maybe misleading for the researcher.

First, it is important to correctly understand why medical scientists favor the hypothesis that health corresponds mostly to one homeostatic state. Indeed, it is not because of some conceptual presupposition, but because of strong factual causes that restrain variability. Some think that we take the most frequently observed form of homeostasis, with all its statistically normal values, to define health *because* it is frequent. In this view, health is stipulated as the most frequent state, which is probably not always beneficial to individuals – what if some are better off with different values than the average, because of some idiosyncrasies? Some think that medical doctors or scientists presuppose that all individuals should have the same blood pressure, level of blood sugar, and so on, because of their concept of health as "statistical normality." This is wrong, as many have noted since Canguilhem. The truth is that there are strong constraints on what material homeostasis can be and how much it can vary. There are so many nested and interlocking systems in an organism that the constraints they put on one another perhaps do not leave so many different possibilities for the organism to survive optimally. The statistical *consequence* is frequency. Conversely, displaying the most frequent form of balance as compared to a population, that is, conformity to a statistical standard of homeostasis, is generally a reliable sign that an organism is healthy. However, material homeostasis is not defined as normal *because* it is frequent, but because the complexity of homeostasis in any organism of the same species does leave some, but not much, room for variability. For this reason, it is often safe to extrapolate from the values generally seen in healthy individuals to the values that correspond to what health should be in one deviant individual. For instance, the level of homeostatic blood pressure can be constitutively higher in an individual, say, due to idiosyncratic variations in the rate of secretion of angiotensin. It is likely that this is a threat to long-term homeostasis because it is unlikely that other idiosyncratic variations counterbalance the risk associated with higher blood pressure. Yet statistically normal values only play a heuristic role in hypothesizing risk: durability of homeostatic state, not statistical deviation, is the reason why the corresponding states are deemed less healthy. Finally, it is important to emphasize that the many constraints on material homeostasis do not make individual variability impossible, but likely to be very limited.

Second, material homeostasis also explains the variability in the *degrees* of health – far from denying that there are such degrees. Indeed, typical organisms of a given species necessarily achieve homeostasis to a certain degree, if they live. They are healthy insofar as they self-maintain, no matter for how many cycles and at what cost to perform them. However, they can be more or less healthy, depending on how long and how robustly they achieve homeostasis. Note that in principle, predictions could be made about the longevity, resistance, and so on, of individual organisms based simply on a thorough understanding of their homeostasis, that is, without any statistical extrapolation from observations on other organisms of the same constitution. For instance, knowing what the formula is for ideal blood pressure to maximize longevity, one could calculate ideal blood pressure for a specific organism with its variations. In other terms, beyond the statistical, heuristic simplification of health, the notion of homeostasis is useful precisely because it can be realized multiply in different organisms (or even in the same organism). Without this notion of homeostasis, differences in performance or longevity would be attributed to the variation of traits rather than to the balance they form together.

Third, there is no presupposition that homeostatic states of an organism should be perfect, or that they all have the same consequences. Indeed, homeostasis seems to imply "integration," that is, coordination of different interlocking systems in the same organism, at the same level or at different levels. An important question is about two (or more) interlocking systems that alternatively balance values so that homeostasis of one disrupts homeostasis of the other. Examples are the suspension of digestion during physical exertion – a fact you are familiar with if you are a long distance runner of the Médoc marathon in France, proposed to drink wine at every stop and eat 12 oysters at kilometer 40 – but also the fact that stress produces immunosuppression, explaining why you are more vulnerable to infection, or the fact that muscular exhaustion happens before fainting due to the priority of the brain over any other part of the organism to receive available glucose from the blood. To be maintained and balanced as such, physical exertion, stress and the activity of the brain require conditions that disrupt other systems. If normal, this situation seems to challenge the material conception of homeostasis and make it a useless abstraction. Indeed, either such a situation is healthy because normal, but not homeostatic, or it is unhealthy because not homeostatic, but normal. In fact, the correct interpretation is not that this is a limitation to the explication of health in terms of homeostasis, but a limitation of health itself due to the constraints of homeostasis. In some cases, an equilibrium results from competition between systems, all of which will function at a suboptimal level. In other cases, one system takes priority over the others. In all cases, trade-offs are involved, which concretely limit what an organism can do or can stand. Health is not *ambiguous* but *limited* because an organism cannot do X and Y at the same time – homeostasis even explains why that is. The normal situation when two systems cannot function optimally at the same time is a limitation of health and the requirements of homeostasis in both systems, and in the system they together form, explain why they cannot.

A qualified notion of homeostasis is even necessary for the researcher to bear in mind that the system they study is never isolated from the rest of the organism.

It is useful to emphasize one last difference between the material and the formal sense of homeostasis regarding nested levels of homeostatic processes.

Homeostasis can indeed be described at various levels. Let us keep in mind here that in the material sense, a "homeostatic" subsystem (cell, tissue, organ, etc.) is a subsystem that participates in homeostasis of the organism. As an example, the size of an adult human *organism* is regulated by simultaneous, antagonistic processes of growth and destruction (Yu et al. 2015). This relies on the homeostatic regulation of the size of *organs* which, in turn, depend on "tissue homeostasis," including the regulation of the number of cells in a tissue. In some tissues, this relies on cell quiescence, that is, a state of balance between growth/proliferation and senescence/apoptosis. Growth and proliferation are under the control of several pathways, one of which is the Hippo pathway, which contains a self-regulatory, negative feedback loop between proteins called YAP/TAZ and LATS1/2. All these processes are homeostatic in some sense. At any of these levels, homeostasis supposedly captures the "health" of the corresponding entity. In many cases, disease is understood as involving a disruption of homeostasis at a given level and, consequently, at higher levels. Typically, the overexpression of liver-specific YAP/TAZ in genetically modified mice leads to a dramatically oversized liver. Conversely, so many diseases have roots in the disruption of cell homeostasis that when a given disease is described as a disruption of homeostasis at a given level, the causes are often investigated in the disruption of homeostasis at the lowest level inside of cells. Thus, in many forms of cancer, YAP/TAZ is found to be overexpressed.

However, a conception of fully nested homeostasis in health and of perfect correspondence, at a given level, between a healthy component and homeostasis in that component is misleading, yet frequently assumed.[12] First, homeostasis at a given level may occur without any significant condition in homeostasis at a lower level and disruption of homeostasis at a given level may not depend on disruption of homeostasis at a lower level. For instance, the regulation of blood pressure indeed depends on the number of cells in the blood (among other things), but it is largely independent from many intracellular mechanisms in blood cells. Besides, many causes of its disruption, like

---

[12] An example is: "The control of each of these variables is dependent on homeostatic control mechanisms that operate at each level (molecular, cellular, tissue, organ, physiological), each contributing to homeostasis at the next level that ultimately translates to vigor at the organismal level" (Ayres 2020).

hemorrhage, do not originate in the disruption of intracellular homeostasis. Second, and more importantly, some forms of homeostasis at a lower level in a system contribute to a disruption of homeostasis at a higher level. For instance, senescent cells are homeostatic in their own way, resisting apoptotic signaling, being pro-inflammatory, and inducing neighboring cells into senescence as well. Generally, homeostasis at this lower level is not defined as the "health" of the corresponding component (e.g., the cell) even if there is, for the cell itself, nothing wrong in the way it works. It is often not even called "homeostasis." Finally, some processes are healthy and not homeostatic at a given level but participate in homeostasis at a higher level. For instance, apoptosis, one of the forms of programmed cell death, is not homeostatic at the level of the cell but is an essential part of "tissue homeostasis" in normal adult tissue. Implicitly, it is then considered that a condition for the health (or even homeostasis) of a component of the organism at level n is that the way it works does not disrupt homeostasis at higher levels (in particular, at the level of the organism). At least four conceptions of health in terms of homeostasis are thus possible:

(1) health of X at level n requires the homeostasis of X at n,
(2) health of X at level n requires one of the homeostatic states (or processes) of X at n that guarantee some homeostatic state (or process) at the level of the organism,
(3) health of X at level n requires a state (or process) of X that guarantees some homeostatic state (or process) at the level of the organism,
(4) health is the state (or process) that results from homeostasis at all lower levels.

Conception (1) relies on the formal definition of homeostasis. Conception (4) wrongly presupposes that health is the balance that results from a series of nicely nested systems, that are all homeostatic. Only conceptions (2) and (3) reflect a relevant conception of material homeostasis. The difference between them depends on whether a component at a level n can be called "healthy" if a non-homeostatic process at this level contributes to homeostasis at the level of the organism. Conception (3) is likely to be preferable.

Homeostasis is often understood as an individual organism's functional state that can last indefinitely. Subsystems that compose this fictional-functional state should be called homeostatic not because they self-maintain, but because they participate in the maintenance of homeostasis. Homeostasis does not necessarily characterize one possible state of the system against all others. It need not be perfect, nor do the multiple homeostatic states of an organism necessarily have the same effects, nor are all the subsystems of the homeostatic state of an organism necessarily self-maintained.

The material concept of homeostasis describes how, in one organism of a given species, the various systems are balanced, nested, integrated, all to a certain, imperfect degree, and with idiosyncratic variations. This set of mutual constraints is called the state of health. In this important sense, health does not disappear, but is impaired in disease. Health is necessary for clinical action. After all, "homeostasis" is less the translation of "health" in physiology, than the explanation of why a certain state should be called "healthy." This concept is not dispensable for physiological research. That said, this subsection should have illustrated how interesting the variations of material homeostasis are, and what an interesting concept it still is for philosophical investigation.

5.5 Health beyond Homeostasis

Many have doubted that the health of living organisms is entirely accounted for by homeostasis. Its focus on the self-maintenance of values within boundaries accounts for how organisms can stand some environmental changes (e.g., thermoregulation and external temperature), but not so obviously how they adapt by changing the reference point of balance. For instance, under the influence of fear, awareness is raised above its normal level, and so is readiness for action – thus shifting the balance of metabolism, neurotransmission, and immunity. This new balance may, of course, still be called homeostatic. But the very ability to shift from one balance to another is a part of health. It has been called "allostasis" (Sterling & Eyer 1988) to insist on the irreducibility of this ability to obtain homeostasis, while others have rejected the term, claiming that the notion of homeostasis already captures this very ability (Day 2005). In a sense, it is not clear that predictive behavioral changes like those induced by fear are not themselves overriding usual levels of homeostasis to re-establish some undetermined, priority balance.

Allostasis has been understood in a formal and in a material sense just like homeostasis. In a formal sense, it is virtually applicable to any homeostatic system that can, temporarily or permanently, change its reference value in adaptation to environmental challenges. This is what largely triggers the dispute about the reducibility of allostasis to homeostasis.

However, the material sense of allostasis has been the most useful to understand the links between behaviors, physiology, mental disorders, health and disease. A clear definition of allostasis in this sense is "regulatory systems in which (1) there is no clear set point, (2) there are individual differences in expression (...), (3) the behavioral and physiological responses are anticipatory (...), and (4) there [is] a vulnerability to physiological overload and the breakdown of regulatory capacities" (Schulkin 2012). The last two points are particularly important. The notion of an anticipatory physiological response focuses on the interlocking of cognitive and physiological processes. Rats build nests when temperature drops, blood pressure increases in anticipation of action, many animals overeat in anticipation of fasting. An anticipatory response does not necessarily involve cognition and can evolve by natural selection (see the example of the water flea in Matthewson & Griffiths 2017). If we call cognition-based anticipatory responses "predictive," we can understand how cognition is rooted in physiology thanks to the notion of allostasis. This also casts light on some aspects of mental health, particularly those associated to the risk of so-called "psychosomatic disorders." Maladapted behaviors of many sorts take a toll on physiology through the protraction of allostatic state – a notion dubbed "allostasis overload" (Korte et al. 2005). Allostasis is a further possibility of adaptation – in this sense, it is just one additional capacity to preserve homeostasis in the long run. Allostatic overload refers to its costs. It has been investigated for itself under the form of a mechanism underpinned by chronically high cortisolemia, the epidemiology of which has been studied (McEwen & Seeman 1999), in association with many diseases and risk factors, some mental, like addiction (Koob & Le Moal 2001), depression and anxiety disorders (McEwen 2007), and others physiological, like obesity, hypertension, and Alzheimer's disease.

Conceptual developments around allostasis may suggest an original conceptualization of mental health. Indeed, two models have been mainly discussed: analogy and integration. By analogy, mental health is the same kind of balanced state as somatic health, only, at a different level. By integration, mental health is a necessary part of health together with somatic health. An example of the latter approach is the biopsychosocial model of health (Bolton & Gillett 2019). With the allostatic model, understood in a material sense, a material hypothesis, grounded in evolution, proposes a conception of how cognition emerged as a mechanism of regulation, but also a view of the necessary trade-offs and risks involved in such a specific form of regulation.

5.6 Health, Fitness, and Evolution

All these developments give substantial support to the hypothesis that health is, indeed, a complex evolved trait – which makes it also an object of investigation for evolutionary biology and philosophy of biology. The investigation of the biological phenomenon of health in the light of evolution remains marginal in medical science, but it is an important conceptual question whether this helps describe basic properties of health. Similar to what was done for disease, let us ask why has health evolved and sketch some conceptual questions raised by evolutionary medicine about health.

At first, it may seem difficult to make a distinction between "health" and the evolutionary concepts of "fitness" or "adaptation." However, "a common misconception is that health and fitness are interchangeable, which is not the case" (Ayres 2020). For instance, in the technical, genetic sense of "fitness" – reproductive success as measured by the increase of the frequency of a gene in a population – health is only one of its components, along with mating success and kin's reproductive success (Stearns & Koella 2008). Also, some physiologists have insisted on homeostasis being a major factor of evolution by natural selection (Turner 2010). To begin with, it is a major constraint on potential mutations – they must certainly make homeostasis evolve in a different direction, but they must also make homeostasis possible in the first place. Another fact is that if health contributes to fitness, it is probably not infrequent that a mutation improves fitness to increase mating success at the expense of health. Thus, a crucial question that has emerged in evolutionary medicine is the study of trade-offs between survival and reproduction but also, more generally, between abilities. The trade-offs evolutionary medicine has investigated are not limited to "positive health" as Boorse presented it (Boorse 1977), that is, innate or acquired individual improvements in abilities beyond the species norm, but they also constitute the species norm of health itself. "Health is commonly perceived as an idealized goal, one that involves optimal bodily function. (...) evolutionary biology offers an insight: concepts of health must incorporate the physiological constraints and ranges of plasticity well documented by the biological community. Those constraints include the idea of trade-offs" (Stearns & Koella 2008).

One important category of trade-offs opposes lifespan and reproduction. In this perspective, the opposite of "health" is not "disease" but, more generally, "degradation," or "aging," understood in a broad sense as the accumulation of damage (Sholl 2021). Another category of trade-offs involves stages of development as they are investigated by life history theory (Gluckman & Hanson 2006a). In this perspective, "health" consists in a predictive strategy of growth, survival, and reproduction over the lifetime. For instance, key hormones such as testosterone, progesterone, estradiol, leptin, and prolactin, are in direct control of these trade-offs, with major impact on health and disease (Bribiescas & Ellison 2007). A third category of trade-offs involves abilities that increase the chances of survival in different environments. Whereas the trade-off between metabolic/muscular function and immune function is often interpreted as an evolutionary trade-off between reproduction and survival, on the presumption that reproduction depends mostly on metabolic and muscular function, it is probably more correct to admit that muscular function can be involved in survival in some circumstances, as much as in sexual competition. Testosterone increases sexual attractiveness, but also metabolic rate in muscle cells by 20 percent in a few seconds.

Here we can only catch a glimpse of the extent of the conceptual questions raised by the evolution of health in general, and human health more specifically. Far from being a simple label for a non-entity – the absence of disease – health is a biological fact that can both be studied by physiology and evolutionary biology, and theorized. In the end, a useful theory of health for medicine must be a theory of the various forms of human health, in comparison with other forms of health in nature.

6 Conclusion

Mostly independently from traditional debates in philosophy of medicine about the definition of terms like "health" and "disease," this Element has developed a philosophical approach to health and disease called the "philosophy of physiology." We diagnosed a problem with philosophy of medicine, namely, a *foundationalist* approach to these concepts, according to which they are immune to changes in biological and medical science, and an exclusive focus on whether *judgments* that something is healthy or pathological are objective, leaving untouched an entire set of conceptual problems in how diseases are scientifically *explained*.

An alternative approach has indeed revealed a set of largely unexplored conceptual questions about disease entities, disease theories, the pathological phenomenon itself, and health. We have emphasized the crucial role of theorization in the explanation of the pathophysiological processes that define disease entities, the existence of partially competing theories to account for an open set of diseases, the possibility of a unified approach to the necessity and universality of the pathological phenomenon, and the existence of an evolved complex trait of health that is not simply the *ens rationis* of "not having any disease."

Theorization is indeed not marginal in medicine. A narrow focus on the part of medical science that consists in clinical trials may suggest that medical science is mostly experimental, pragmatic, and atheoretical. Evidence-based medicine (EBM) is a powerful research agenda that has emphasized the importance of establishing clinical facts – typically, does a drug *really* work? – and not take the existence of a theory – from which it can be inferred that a drug should work – for evidence of a clinical fact. Fairly enough, philosophers of EBM have revealed, emphasized, and discussed the theory of causality that EBM necessarily requires (Russo & Williamson 2007). However, other philosophers have insisted on the role of formalized models of physiological and pathophysiological processes in medical science (Thompson 2011). Physiology may be considered a field of *intensive* theorization – specific diseases, disease types, and even the pathological phenomenon itself, are the object of frequent attempts of explanation and prediction through causal formalization of the process(es) that specifically constitutes them. Physiological theories may be of a special type, as was already suggested a long time ago (Schaffner 1986). *One* theory may one day explain *all* diseases. Either way, these are not premises of philosophy of physiology. What is is that philosophy of physiology sets itself a different goal from traditional philosophy of medicine about specific diseases, disease theories and the concept of disease. In philosophy of medicine, the ultimate goal of the conceptual work on diseases, disease or health, has always been social and ethical – in the end, it is about judgments and actions. In philosophy of physiology, the goal of all conceptual work is to push further our understanding of the natural phenomena of health and diseases. It is about explanations and predictions of the world of health and disease.

References

Akira, S., Uematsu, S., & Takeuchi, O. (2006). Pathogen recognition and innate immunity. *Cell*, **124**(4), 783–801.

American Psychiatric Association. (1987). *Diagnostic and Statistical Manual of Mental Disorders: DSM-III-R*, Washington, D.C.: American Psychiatric Assoc.

American Psychiatric Association. (2000). *Diagnostic and Statistical Manual of Mental Disorders, Text Revision (DSM-IV-TR)*, Washington, D.C.: American Psychiatric Association.

Ayres, J. S. (2020). The biology of physiological health. *Cell*, **181**, 250–269.

Barker, D. (1986). Infant mortality, childhood nutrition, and ischaemic heart disease in England and Wales. *The Lancet*, **327**(8489), 1077–1081.

Bateson, P., Barker, D., Clutton-Brock, T. et al. (2004). Developmental plasticity and human health. *Nature*, **430**(6998), 419–421.

Becsei-Kilborn, E. (2010). Scientific discovery and scientific reputation: The reception of Peyton Rous' discovery of the chicken sarcoma virus. *Journal of the History of Biology*, **43**(1), 111–157.

Belkaid, Y., & Hand, T. W. (2014). Role of the microbiota in immunity and inflammation. *Cell*, **157**(1), 121–141.

Bernard-Weil, E. (1999). Pathological homeostasis: Its meaning, its inferences. *Medical Hypotheses*, **53**(1), 24–31.

Bertalanffy, L. von. (1969). *General System Theory: Foundations, Development, Applications*, New York: G. Braziller.

Bolton, D., & Gillett, G. (2019). *The Biopsychosocial Model of Health and Disease: New Philosophical and Scientific Developments*, Cham: Springer International. https://doi.org/10.1007/978-3-030-11899-0.

Boorse, C. (1975). On the distinction between disease and illness. *Philosophy and Public Affairs*, **5**(1), 49–68.

Boorse, C. (1977). Health as a theoretical concept. *Philosophy of Science*, **44**(4), 542–573.

Boorse, C. (1997). A rebuttal on health. In J. M. Humber & R. F. Almeder, eds., *What Is Disease?* Totowa, NJ: Humana Press, pp. 1–134.

Botstein, D., & Risch, N. (2003). Discovering genotypes underlying human phenotypes: Past successes for Mendelian disease, future approaches for complex disease. *Nature Genetics*, **33**(S3), 228–237.

Bourrat, P., & Griffiths, P. E. (2021). The idea of mismatch in evolutionary medicine. *The British Journal for the Philosophy of Science*, 716543.

Bribiescas, R. G., & Ellison, P. T. (2007). How hormones mediate trade-offs in human health and disease. In S. C. Stearns & J. C. Koella, eds., *Evolution in Health and Disease*, New York: Oxford University Press, pp. 77–94.

Bugianesi, E., Gastaldelli, A., Vanni, E. et al. (2005). Insulin resistance in non-diabetic patients with non-alcoholic fatty liver disease: Sites and mechanisms. *Diabetologia*, **48**(4), 634–642.

Campisi, J. (2013). Aging, cellular senescence, and cancer. *Annual Review of Physiology*, **75**, 685–705.

Canguilhem, G. (1991). *The Normal and the Pathological*, New edition, Translated by Carolyn R. Fawcett, New York: Zone Books.

Cannon, W. B. (1929). Organization for physiological homeostasis. *Physiological Reviews*, **9**(3), 399–431.

Conrad, P. (2007). *The Medicalization of Society: On the Transformation of Human Conditions into Treatable Disorders*, 1st ed., Baltimore, MD: Johns Hopkins University Press.

Cooper, R. (2005). *Classifying Madness: A Philosophical Examination of the Diagnostic and Statistical Manual of Mental Disorders*, Dordrecht: Springer.

Cooper, R. (2007). *Psychiatry and Philosophy of Science*, Stockfield: McGill-Queen's University Press.

Cournoyea, M. (2013). Ancestral assumptions and the clinical uncertainty of evolutionary medicine. *Perspectives in Biology and Medicine*, **56**(1), 36–52.

Craver, C. F. (2009). Mechanisms and natural kinds. *Philosophical Psychology*, **22**(5), 575–594.

Cryan, J. F., O'Riordan, K. J., Cowan, C. S. M. et al. (2019). The microbiota-gut-brain axis. *Physiological Reviews*, **99**(4), 1877–2013.

Clouser, K. D., Culver, C. M., & Gert, B. (1981). Malady – A new treatment of disease. *Hastings Center Report*, **11**(3), 29–37. https://doi.org/10.2307/3561321.

Darrason, M. (2013). Unifying diseases from a genetic point of view: The example of the genetic theory of infectious diseases. *Theoretical Medicine and Bioethics*, **34**, 327–344.

Day, T. A. (2005). Defining stress as a prelude to mapping its neurocircuitry: No help from allostasis. *Progress in Neuro-Psychopharmacology and Biological Psychiatry*, **29**(8), 1195–1200.

de Magalhães, J. P. (2022). Every gene can (and possibly will) be associated with cancer. *Trends in Genetics*, **38**(3), 216–217.

de Vos, W. M., & de Vos, E. A. (2012). Role of the intestinal microbiome in health and disease: From correlation to causation. *Nutrition Reviews*, **70**, S45–S56.

Deanfield, J. E., Halcox, J. P., & Rabelink, T. J. (2007). Endothelial function and dysfunction: Testing and clinical relevance. *Circulation*, **115**(10), 1285–1295.

Dussault, A. C., & Gagné-Julien, A.-M. (2015). Health, homeostasis, and the situation-specificity of normality. *Theoretical Medicine and Bioethics*, **36**(1), 61–81.

Ekbom, A., Adami, H.-O., Trichopoulos, D., Hsieh, C.-C., & Lan, S.-J. (1992). Evidence of prenatal influences on breast cancer risk. *The Lancet*, **340**(8826), 1015–1018.

Engelhardt, H. T. (1996). *The Foundations of Bioethics*, New York: Oxford University Press.

Ereshefsky, M. (2009). Defining "health" and "disease." *Studies in History and Philosophy of Science Part C: Studies in History and Philosophy of Biological and Biomedical Sciences*, **40**(3), 221–227.

Fleming, T., Watkins, A., Velazquez, M. et al. (2018). Origins of lifetime health around the time of conception: Causes and consequences. *The Lancet* **391** (10132), 1842–1852. https://doi.org/10.1016/S0140-6736(18)30312-X.

Fodor, J. A. (1974). Special sciences (or: The disunity of science as a working hypothesis). *Synthese*, **28**(2), 97–115.

Frank, S. A. (1996). Models of parasite virulence. *The Quarterly Review of Biology*, **71**(1), 37–78.

Fuller, J. (2018). What are chronic diseases? *Synthese*, **195**, 3197–3220.

Galen. (1991). *On the Therapeutic Method*. (R. J. Hankinson, Trans.). New York: Oxford University Press.

Giaimo, S., & d'Adda di Fagagna, F. (2012). Is cellular senescence an example of antagonistic pleiotropy?: Cellular senescence and antagonistic pleiotropy. *Aging Cell*, **11**(3), 378–383.

Gluckman, P. D., Beedle, A., & Hanson, M. A. (2009). *Principles of Evolutionary Medicine*, Oxford: Oxford University Press.

Gluckman, P. D., & Hanson, M. A. (2006a). The developmental origins of health and disease. In E. M. Wintour & J. A. Owens, eds., *Early Life Origins of Health and Disease*, Vol. 573, Boston, MA: Springer, pp. 1–7.

Gluckman, P., & Hanson, M. (Eds.). (2006b). *Developmental Origins of Health and Disease*, Cambridge: Cambridge University Press. https://doi.org/10.1017/CBO9780511544699.

Goel, P. (2015). Insulin resistance or hypersecretion? The βIG picture revisited. *Journal of Theoretical Biology*, **384**, 131–139.

Greslehner, G. P. (2020). Microbiome structure and function: A new framework for interpreting data. *BioEssays*, **42**(7), 1900255, 1–8.

Griffiths, P. E., & Matthewson, J. (2016). Evolution, dysfunction, and disease: A reappraisal. *The British Journal for the Philosophy of Science*, **69**, 301–327.

Grmek, M. (1969). Préliminaires d'une étude historique des maladies. *Annales*, **24**(6), 1473–1483.

Hajishengallis, G., Darveau, R. P., & Curtis, M. A. (2012). The keystone-pathogen hypothesis. *Nature Reviews Microbiology*, **10**(10), 717–725.

Hansson, G. K., & Libby, P. (2006). The immune response in atherosclerosis: A double-edged sword. *Nature Reviews Immunology*, **6**(7), 508–519.

Hausman, D. M. (2011). Is an overdose of paracetamol bad for one's health? *The British Journal for the Philosophy of Science*, **62**(3), 657–668.

Hausman, D. M. (2012). Measuring or valuing population health: Some conceptual problems. *Public Health Ethics*, **5**(3), 229–239.

Heikkila, K., Nyberg, S. T., Theorell, T. et al. for the IPD-Work Consortium. (2013). Work stress and risk of cancer: Meta-analysis of 5700 incident cancer events in 116 000 European men and women. *British Medical Journal*, **346** (feb07 1), f165–f165.

Heim, C., Newport, D. J., Mletzko, T., Miller, A. H., & Nemeroff, C. B. (2008). The link between childhood trauma and depression: Insights from HPA axis studies in humans. *Psychoneuroendocrinology*, **33**(6), 693–710.

Helzer, J. E., Kraemer, H. C., & Krueger, R. F. (Eds.). (2008). *Dimensional Approaches in Diagnostic Classification: Refining the Research Agenda for DSM-V*. Arlington, VA: American Psychiatric Publishing.

Heneka, M. T., Kummer, M. P., & Latz, E. (2014). Innate immune activation in neurodegenerative disease. *Nature Reviews Immunology*, **14**(7), 463–477.

Heppner, F. L., Ransohoff, R. M., & Becher, B. (2015). Immune attack: The role of inflammation in Alzheimer disease. *Nature Reviews Neuroscience*, **16**(6), 358–372.

Hesslow, G. (1984). What is a genetic disease? In L. Nordenfelt & B. I. B. Lindahl, eds., *Health, Disease and Causal Explanation in Medicine*, Dordrecht, Holland: Reidel, pp. 183–193.

Hesslow, G. (1993). Do we need a concept of disease? *Theoretical Medicine and Bioethics*, **14**(1), 1–14. https://doi.org/10.1007/BF00993984.

Hofmann, B. (2005). Simplified models of the relationship between health and disease. *Theoretical Medicine and Bioethics*, **26**(5), 355–377.

Honda, K., & Littman, D. R. (2016). The microbiota in adaptive immune homeostasis and disease. *Nature*, **535**(7610), 75–84.

Hooks, K. B., & O'Malley, M. A. (2017). Dysbiosis and its discontents. *mBio*, **8**(5), mBio.01492–17, e01492–17.

Hucklenbroich, P. (2014). "Disease entity" as the key theoretical concept of medicine. *Journal of Medicine and Philosophy*, **39**(6), 609–633.

Jucker, M., & Walker, L. C. (2013). Self-propagation of pathogenic protein aggregates in neurodegenerative diseases. *Nature*, **501**(7465), 45–51.

Kannisto, V. (1991). Frailty and survival. *Genus*, **47**(3/4), 101–118.

Karatsoreos, I. N., & McEwen, B. S. (2011). Psychobiological allostasis: Resistance, resilience and vulnerability. *Trends in Cognitive Sciences*, **15**(12), 576–584.

Kendell, R., & Jablensky, A. (2003). Distinguishing between the validity and utility of psychiatric diagnoses. *The American Journal of Psychiatry*, **160**(1), 4–12.

Kershnar, S. (2016). Quantifying health across populations. *Bioethics*, **30**(6), 451–461.

Keuck, L. K., & Hauswald, R. (2016). Indeterminacy in medical classification: On continuity, interest-relativity, and vagueness. In K. Geert, L. K. Keuck, & R. Hauswald, eds., *Gradualist Approaches to Mental Health and Disease*, Oxford: Oxford University Press, pp. 93–116.

Kingma, E. (2007). What is it to be healthy? *Analysis*, **67**(294), 128–133.

Kingma, E. (2010). Paracetamol, poison, and polio: Why Boorse's account of function fails to distinguish health and disease. *British Journal for the Philosophy of Science*, **61**(2), 241–264.

Kingma, E. (2016). Situation-specific disease and dispositional function. *The British Journal for the Philosophy of Science*, **67**(2): 391–404. https://doi.org/10.1093/bjps/axu041.

Kirkwood, T. (1977). Evolution of aging. *Nature*, **270**(5635), 301–304.

Kirkwood, T. B. L., & Holliday, R. (1979). The evolution of ageing and longevity. *Proceedings of the Royal Society of London. Series B. Biological Sciences*, **205**(1161), 531–546.

Koeth, R. A., Wang, Z., Levison, B. S. et al. (2013). Intestinal microbiota metabolism of l-carnitine, a nutrient in red meat, promotes atherosclerosis. *Nature Medicine*, **19**(5), 576–585.

Koob, G. F., & Le Moal, M. (2001). Drug addiction, dysregulation of reward, and allostasis. *Neuropsychopharmacology: Official Publication of the American College of Neuropsychopharmacology*, **24**(2), 97–129.

Korte, S. M., Koolhaas, J. M., Wingfield, J. C., & McEwen, B. S. (2005). The Darwinian concept of stress: Benefits of allostasis and costs of allostatic load and the trade-offs in health and disease. *Neuroscience & Biobehavioral Reviews*, **29**(1), 3–38.

Kotas, M. E., & Medzhitov, R. (2015). Homeostasis, inflammation, and disease susceptibility. *Cell*, **160**(5), 816–827.

Lemoine, M. (2009). The meaning of the opposition between the healthy and the pathological and its consequences. *Medicine, Health Care, and Philosophy*, **12**(3), 355–362.

Lemoine, M. (2013). Defining disease beyond conceptual analysis: An analysis of conceptual analysis in philosophy of medicine. *Theoretical Medicine and Bioethics*, **34**(4), 309–325.

Lemoine, M. (2014). The naturalization of the concept of disease. In G. Lambert, M. Silberstein, & P. Huneman, eds., *Classification, Disease and Evidence: New Essays in the Philosophy of Medicine*, Amsterdam: Springer, pp. 19–41.

Lemoine, M. (2016). Molecular complexity: Why has psychiatry not been revolutionized by genomics (yet)? In G. Boniolo & M. J. Nathan, eds., *Philosophical Foundations of Molecular Medicine*, Dordrecht: Springer, pp. 81–99.

Lemoine, M. (2020). Defining aging. *Biology & Philosophy*, **35**(5), 46.

Lemoine, M., & Giroux, É. (2016). Is Boorse's biostatistical theory of health naturalistic? In É. Giroux, ed., *Naturalism in the Philosophy of Health*, Vol 17, Switzerland: Springer, pp. 19–38.

Lemoine, M., & Pradeu, T. (2018). Dissecting the meanings of "physiology" to assess the vitality of the discipline. *Physiology (Bethesda, Md.)*, **33**(4), 236–245.

Liu, K. E., Love, A. C., & Travisano, M. (2016). How cancer spread: Reconceptualizing a disease. In G. Boniolo & M. J. Nathan, eds., *Philosophy of Molecular Medicine*, New York: Routledge, pp. 100–121.

Lock, M. M. (2013). *The Alzheimer conundrum: Entanglements of Dementia and Aging*, Princeton, TX: Princeton University Press.

López-Otín, C., & Kroemer, G. (2021). Hallmarks of health. *Cell*, **184**(1), 33-63. https://doi.org/10.1016/j.cell.2020.11.034.

Loscalzo, J., Kohane, I., & Barabasi, A.-L. (2007). Human disease classification in the postgenomic era: A complex systems approach to human pathobiology. *Molecular Systems Biology*, **3**, 1–11.

Lynch, K. E., Parke, E. C., & O'Malley, M. A. (2019). How causal are microbiomes? A comparison with the Helicobacter pylori explanation of ulcers. *Biology & Philosophy*, **34**(6), 62.

Magnus, D. (2004). The concept of genetic disease. In A. L. Caplan, J. J. McCartney, & D. A. Sisti, eds., *Health, Disease and Illness: Concepts in Medicine*, Washington, DC: Georgetown University Press, pp. 233–242.

Maj, M., & Gaebel, W. (2002). *Psychiatric Diagnosis and Classification*, Chichester: John Wiley.

Matthews, D. R., Hosker, J. R., Rudenski, A. S. et al. (1985). Homeostasis model assessment: Insulin resistance and fl-cell function from fasting plasma glucose and insulin concentrations in man. *Diabetologia*, **28**, 412–419.

Matthewson, J., & Griffiths, P. E. (2017). Biological criteria of disease: Four ways of going wrong. *The Journal of Medicine and Philosophy: A Forum for Bioethics and Philosophy of Medicine*, **42**(4), 447–466.

McEwen, B. S. (2007). Physiology and neurobiology of stress and adaptation: Central role of the brain. *Physiological Reviews*, **87**(3), 873–904.

McEwen, B. S., Bowles, N. P., Gray, J. D. et al. (2015). Mechanisms of stress in the brain. *Nature Neuroscience*, **18**(10), 1353–1363.

McEwen, B. S., & Seeman, T. (1999). Protective and damaging effects of mediators of stress: Elaborating and testing the concepts of allostasis and allostatic load. *Annals of the New York Academy of Sciences*, **896**(1), 30–47.

Medzhitov, R., Schneider, D. S., & Soares, M. P. (2012). Disease tolerance as a defense strategy. *Science*, **335**(6071), 936–941.

Méthot, P.-O. (2011). Research traditions and evolutionary explanations in medicine. *Theoretical Medicine and Bioethics*, **32**(1), 75–90.

Méthot, P.-O., & Alizon, S. (2014). What is a pathogen? Toward a process view of host-parasite interactions. *Virulence*, **5**(8), 775–785.

Miles, J. A., Davies, T. A., Hayman, R. D. et al. (2020). A case study of eukaryogenesis: The evolution of photoreception by photolyase/cryptochrome proteins. *Journal of Molecular Evolution*, **88**(8–9), 662–673.

Millon, T., Krueger, R. F., & Simonsen, E. (2010). *Contemporary Directions in Psychopathology: Scientific Foundations of the DSM-V and ICD-11*, New York: Guilford.

Murphy, D., & Woolfolk, R. L. (2000). Conceptual analysis versus scientific understanding: An assessment of wakefield's folk psychiatry. *Philosophy, Psychiatry, and Psychology*, **7**(4), 271–293.

Nervi, M. (2010). Mechanisms, malfunctions and explanation in medicine. *Biology and Philosophy*, **25**(2), 215–228.

Nesse, R. M. (2001). On the difficulty of defining disease: A Darwinian perspective. *Medicine, Health Care and Philosophy*, **4**(1), 37–46.

Nordenfelt, L. Y. (1995). *On the Nature of Health: An Action-Theoretic Approach*, 2nd ed., Dordrecht: Springer.

Olesen, S. W., & Alm, E. J. (2016). Dysbiosis is not an answer. *Nature Microbiology*, **1**(12), 1–2, 16228.

Olshansky, S. J. (2010). The law of mortality revisited: Interspecies comparisons of mortality. *Journal of Comparative Pathology*, **142**(Suppl 1), S4–S9.

Osborn, O., & Olefsky, J. M. (2012). The cellular and signaling networks linking the immune system and metabolism in disease. *Nature Medicine*, **18**(3), 363–374.

Pradeu, T., Lemoine, M., Khelfaoui, M., & Gingras, Y. (2024). Philosophy in science: Can philosophers of science permeate through science and produce scientific knowledge? *The British Journal for the Philosophy of Science*, **75**(2), 375–416. https://doi.org/10.1086/715518.

Qin, J., Li, Y., Cai, Z. et al. (2012). A metagenome-wide association study of gut microbiota in type 2 diabetes. *Nature*, **490**(7418), 55–60.

Raibley, J. (2013). Health and well-being. *Philosophical Studies*, **165**(2), 469–489.

Reiche, E. M. V., Nunes, S. O. V., & Morimoto, H. K. (2004). Stress, depression, the immune system, and cancer. *The Lancet Oncology*, **5**(10), 617–625.

Routy, B., Le Chatelier, E., Derosa, L. et al. (2018). Gut microbiome influences efficacy of PD-1–based immunotherapy against epithelial tumors. *Science*, **359**(6371), 91–97.

Russo, F., & Williamson, J. (2007). Interpreting causality in the health sciences. *International Studies in the Philosophy of Science*, **21**(2), 157–170.

Sadegh-Zadeh, K. (1999). Fundamentals of clinical methodology: 3. Nosology. *Artificial Intelligence in Medicine*, **17**(1), 87–108.

Sadegh-Zadeh, K. (2008). A prototype resemblance theory of disease. *Journal of Medicine and Philosophy*, **33**, 106–139.

Sadegh-Zadeh, K. (2012). *Handbook of Analytic Philosophy of Medicine*, Dordrecht: Springer.

Schaffner, K. F. (1986). Exemplar reasoning about biological models and diseases: A relation between the philosophy of medicine and philosophy of science. *Journal of Medicine and Philosophy*, **11**(1), 63–80.

Schermer, M. H. N. (2023). Preclinical disease or risk factor? Alzheimer's disease as a case study of changing conceptualizations of disease. *The Journal of Medicine and Philosophy: A Forum for Bioethics and Philosophy of Medicine*, **48**(4), 322–334.

Schreiber, R. D., Old, L. J., & Smyth, M. J. (2011). Cancer immunoediting: Integrating immunity's roles in cancer suppression and promotion. *Science*, **331**(6024), 1565–1570.

Schulkin, J. (2012). *Allostasis, Homeostasis, and the Costs of Physiological Adaptation*, Reprint, Cambridge: Cambridge University Press.

Schwabe, R. F., & Jobin, C. (2013). The microbiome and cancer. *Nature Reviews Cancer*, **13**(11), 800–812.

Schwartz, P. H. (2007). Decision and discovery in defining "disease." In H. Kincaid & J. McKitrick, eds., *Establishing Medical Reality*, Amsterdam: Springer, pp. 47–63.

Severinsen, M. (2001). Principles behind definitions of diseases – a criticism of the principle of disease mechanism and the development of a pragmatic alternative. *Theoretical Medicine and Bioethics*, **22**(4): 319–336. https://doi.org/10.1023/A:1011830602137.

Shokeir, M. H. K. (1975). Investigation on Huntington's disease in the Canadian Prairies: II. Fecundity and Fitness. *Clinical Genetics*, **7**(4), 349–353.

Sholl, J. (2020). The sciences of healthy aging await a theory of health. *Biogerontology*, **21**(3), 399–409.

Sholl, J. (2021). Can aging research generate a theory of health? *History and Philosophy of the Life Sciences*, **43**(2), 45.

Sholl, J., & Okholm, S. (2021). Taking a naturalistic turn in the health and disease debate. *Teorema*, **40**(1), 91–109.

Sholl, J., & Rattan, S. I. S. (Eds.). (2020). *Explaining Health across the Sciences*, Vol. 12, Cham: Springer International. https://doi.org/10.1007/978-3-030-52663-4.

Sholl, J., Sepich-Poore, G. D., Knight, R., & Pradeu, T. (2021). Redrawing therapeutic boundaries: Microbiota and cancer. *Trends in Cancer*, **8**(2), 87–97.

Smith, K. C. (2001). A disease by any other name: Musings on the concept of a genetic disease. *Medicine, Health Care and Philosophy*, **4**(1), 19–30.

Solomon, M., Simon, J. R., & Kincaid, H. (Eds.). (2017). *The Routledge Companion to Philosophy of Medicine*, New York: Routledge, Taylor & Francis Group.

Stearns, S. C., & Koella, J. C. (2008). *Evolution in Health and Disease*, 2nd ed., New York: Oxford University Press.

Steptoe, A., & Kivimäki, M. (2012). Stress and cardiovascular disease. *Nature Reviews Cardiology*, **9**(6), 360–370.

Sterling, P., & Eyer, J. (1988). Allostasis: A new paradigm to explain arousal pathology. In S. Fisher & J. Reason, eds., *Handbook of Life Stress, Cognition and Health*. New York: John Wiley & Sons, pp. 629–649.

Szymanska, H., Lechowska-Piskorowska, J., Krysiak, E. et al. (2014). Neoplastic and nonneoplastic lesions in aging mice of unique and common inbred strains contribution to modeling of human neoplastic diseases. *Veterinary Pathology*, **51**(3), 663–679.

Tabb, K. (2015). Psychiatric progress and the assumption of diagnostic discrimination. *Philosophy of Science*, **82**, 1047–1058.

Tabb, K. (2020). Should psychiatry be precise? Reduction, big data, and nosological revision in mental health research. In K. S. Kendler, J. Parnas, & P. Zachar, eds., *Levels of Analysis in Psychopathology*, 1st ed., New York: Cambridge University Press, pp. 308–334.

Thagard, P. (1999). *How Scientists Explain Disease*, Princeton: New Ed, Princeton University Press.

Thompson, R. P. (2011). Models and theories in medicine. In F. Gifford, ed., *Philosophy of Medicine*, Oxford: Elsevier, pp. 115–136.

Thun, M. J., Linet, M. S., Cerhan, J. R., Haiman, C., & Schottenfeld, D. (Eds.). (2018). *Cancer Epidemiology and Prevention*, 4th ed., New York: Oxford University Press.

Tremaroli, V., & Bäckhed, F. (2012). Functional interactions between the gut microbiota and host metabolism. *Nature*, **489**(7415), 242–249.

Tsou, J. Y. (2012). Intervention, causal reasoning, and the neurobiology of mental disorders: Pharmacological drugs as experimental instruments. *Studies in History and Philosophy of Science Part C*, **43**(2), 542–551.

Turner, J. S. (2010). *The Tinkererer's Accomplice: How Design Emerges from Life Itself*, Cambridge, MA: Harvard University Press.

Valles, S. A. (2018). *Philosophy of Population Health Science: Philosophy for a New Public Health Era*, New York: Routledge, Taylor & Francis Group.

Venkatapuram, S. (2013). Health, vital goals, and central human capabilities. *Bioethics*, **27**(5), 271–279.

Viau, V. (2002). Functional cross-talk between the hypothalamic-pituitary-gonadal and -adrenal axes: Testosterone and corticosterone interact on HPA function. *Journal of Neuroendocrinology*, **14**(6), 506–513.

Virgin, H. W., Wherry, E. J., & Ahmed, R. (2009). Redefining chronic viral infection. *Cell*, **138**(1), 30–50.

Vogelstein, B., & Kinzler, K. W. (2004). Cancer genes and the pathways they control. *Nature Medicine*, **10**(8), 11, 30–50.

Wachter, K. W. (2008). Biodemography comes of age. *Demographic Research*, **19**, 1501–1512.

Wakefield, J. C. (1992). The concept of mental disorder: On the boundary between biological facts and social values. *American Psychologist*, **47**(3), 373–388.

Webster, J. I., Tonelli, L., & Sternberg, E. M. (2002). Neuroendocrine regulation of immunity. *Annual Review of Immunology*, **20**(1), 125–163.

Wellcome Trust Case Control Consortium. (2007). Genome-wide association study of 14,000 cases of seven common diseases and 3,000 shared controls. *Nature*, **447**(7145), 661–678.

Whitbeck, C. (1977). Causation in medicine: The disease entity model. *Philosophy of Science*, **44**(4), 619–637.

Whitbeck, C. (1981). A theory of health. In A. L. Caplan, H. T. Engelhardt, & J. J. McCartney, eds., *Concepts of Health and Disease: Interdisciplinary Perspectives*, Reading, MA: Addison-Wesley, Advanced Book Program/World Science Division, pp. 611–626.

Wiener, N. (1948). *Cybernetics: Or Control and Communication in the Animal and the Machine*, Paris, France: Hermann.

Williams, G. C. (1957). Pleiotropy, natural selection, and the evolution of senescence. *Evolution*, **11**(4), 398–411.

Williams, G., & Nesse, R. (1991). The dawn of Darwinian medicine. *Quarterly Review of Biology*, **66**(1), 1–22.

Worrall, J., & Worrall, J. (2001). Defining disease: Much ado about nothing? In A.-T. Tymieniecka & E. Agazzi, eds., *Life Interpretation and the Sense of Illness within the Human Condition*, Netherlands: Springer, pp. 33–55.

Yu, F.-X., Zhao, B., & Guan, K.-L. (2015). Hippo pathway in organ size control, tissue homeostasis, and cancer. *Cell*, **163**(4), 811–828.

Acknowledgments

Steeves Demazeux, Jan Pieter Konsman, Simon Okholm, Thomas Pradeu, and Jonathan Sholl have read the first draft of this Element and have added eight months of delay to my workload. Thanks, guys. Really. Jonathan Sholl has kindly edited the final manuscript and made even more useful suggestions.

Cambridge Elements ≡

Philosophy of Biology

Grant Ramsey
KU Leuven

Grant Ramsey is a BOFZAP research professor at the Institute of Philosophy, KU Leuven, Belgium. His work centers on philosophical problems at the foundation of evolutionary biology. He has been awarded the Popper Prize twice for his work in this area. He also publishes in the philosophy of animal behavior, human nature and the moral emotions. He runs the Ramsey Lab (theramseylab.org), a highly collaborative research group focused on issues in the philosophy of the life sciences.

About the Series

This Cambridge Elements series provides concise and structured introductions to all of the central topics in the philosophy of biology. Contributors to the series are cutting-edge researchers who offer balanced, comprehensive coverage of multiple perspectives, while also developing new ideas and arguments from a unique viewpoint.

Cambridge Elements

Philosophy of Biology

Elements in the Series

Biological Individuality
Alison K. McConwell

Human Nature
Grant Ramsey

Ecological Complexity
Alkistis Elliott-Graves

Units of Selection
Javier Suárez and Elisabeth A. Lloyd

Evolution and Development: Conceptual Issues
Alan C. Love

Inclusive Fitness and Kin Selection
Hannah Rubin

Animal Models of Human Disease
Sara Green

Cultural Selection
Tim Lewens

Controlled Experiments
Jutta Schickore

Explanation in Biology
Lauren N. Ross

Biological Organization
Leonardo Bich

Philosophy of Physiology
Maël Lemoine

A full series listing is available at: www.cambridge.org/EPBY

For EU product safety concerns, contact us at Calle de José Abascal, 56–1°, 28003 Madrid, Spain or eugpsr@cambridge.org.

www.ingramcontent.com/pod-product-compliance
Lightning Source LLC
LaVergne TN
LVHW020350260326
834688LV00045B/1650